LANDS OF BRIGHTER DESTINY:

THE PUBLIC LANDS
OF THE AMERICAN WEST

FULCRUM ᴵⁿᶜ.

LANDS OF BRIGHTER DESTINY

THE PUBLIC LANDS OF THE AMERICAN WEST

ELIZABETH DARBY JUNKIN

PHOTOGRAPHY BY JAMES COOK

FULCRUM
GOLDEN, COLORADO 1986

Book Design by Bob Schram
Cover Art by Patricia Sullivan

LIBRARY OF CONGRESS CATALOGING-IN-PUBLICATION DATA

Junkin, Elizabeth Darby
Lands of Brighter Destiny.

Bibliography: p.
Includes index.
1. West (U.S.)--Public lands. 2. Alaska--Public
lands.   I. Title.
HD243.A17J86 1986   333.1'0978   86-4814
ISBN 1-55591-000-9

FULCRUM, INC.
GOLDEN, COLORADO

*For my family
and Ted*

TABLE OF CONTENTS

FOREWORD

"But the great fact was the land itself, which seemed to overwhelm the little beginnings of human society that struggled in its somber wastes. It was from facing this vast hardness that the boy's mouth had become so bitter; because he felt that men were too weak to make any mark here, that the land wanted to be let alone, to preserve its own fierce strength, its peculiar, savage kind of beauty, its uninterrupted mournfulness.

Willa Cather
1913*

"Without any remaining wilderness, we are committed wholly, without chance for even momentary reflection and rest, to a headlong drive into our technological termite-life, the Brave New World of a completely man-controlled environment. We need wilderness preserved — as much of it as is still left, and as many kinds — because it was the challenge against which our character as a people was formed."

Wallace Stegner
1961**

As I sat on the rocky bank, I watched a thousand years of the life and the rhythms of survival pass during one sunset; a thousand moments of evolution and creation marching forward to this one moment of life and death. The time passed invisibly before my eyes, destruction and creation in the one eternity and one millisecond I observed on the hill overlooking the Toklat River. It was nourishment of life itself, by life feeding on life just as the dark rolled into dusk and then on, into new days. It was around me, moving forward; within me, captured for a lifetime in my wonder; beyond me, in that

I had no immediate part in it, save as witness to the force of time and nature itself. A part of me felt as the caribou that lay on the banks of the river, now three days dead with a grizzly sow glutted on his body and sleeping soundly on his back while her cubs wrestled near by. His rack of antlers glowed in the golden twilight, bloodied and vibrating red with the velvet of summer's bounty still covering them. His fate was unknown to him yet simultaneously fulfilled, he now lay opened to the bears, eventually to the wolf, to scavengers, to nature and to the movement of time that created him, nourished him and utilized him.

I wondered what use will there be of my words and thoughts, passion and care for this land that is my home? What is the purpose of this expression of my concern and will I know if I have fulfilled it? Or will the results of this expression become apparent only with my passing, after I have relinquished to time a nature the materials I was loaned to use during my life?

When I began this book, I saw it as a chance to treat a "major Western issue." As a journalist, I had covered the western topics such as the Sagebrush Rebellion and natural resource issues and had long been aware of the vast amount of land that is in the public domain around my home, the West. I was curious about what was actually out there, beyond the forests I had hiked or the national parks and wilderness I had visited as a child as part of the traditional summer auto-vacations. I was curious about the "issues" that were facing the management of this land and curious about how — or whether — these issues were being resolved. I looked at the land as an object, as property, as an issue, as a political concern, much as one does in covering any breaking news: devoid of feeling, much as the agencies which manage the land do. Just the facts, please. A land described in statistics and numbers, much as a human tragedy is described in statistics and casualties rather than human deaths and sadness.

As I've come to finish this book, I have become unwillingly plunged into the realization of the vitalness of this western land, seeing it finally not as an object, nor as merely property, but as something that we simply cannot live without. I have come to see that the human tragedy is that we look at the land in statistics and numbers, objectifying and eventually quantifying the casualties of our own apathy rather than seeing it as being vibrantly necessary. The land is the pinion of our lives and of our very existence. The "issues" affecting the land are a part of the issues facing us on a daily basis. Life and death of the land is life and death of us, as individuals, societal and as a civilization.

What is land, but the chance to witness our past and present simultaneously? Without land, we have no foundation, no tradition. In essence, we don't exist save for the temporary moment of the present. But land is also the chance to see our future. It — and our judicious care of the land, during our tenure of it — is the basis of our immortality, not the structures we build upon it. Without it, we have no future, no place to go, no place to plant our hopes and no material, no resources to rely upon. The land is not merely property; it is the fabric of our lives. Without it, we become paupers in the only home we shall ever know. By ignoring the purposes of our use of it, we make ourselves homeless through our own intemperance.

As others have noted, we do live in a complicated world, mostly because we have little to do with our direct survival. Unlike the bear or wolf or caribou I witnessed in Alaska, whose main Autumnal task is to consume food in order to gain body weight for winter survival, our daily concerns in Autumn revolve around our work, so that we may receive our pay, so that we may buy nourishment and shelter for our families. We are separated from the land by many layers of tasks and so become distant in our understanding and thus distant from the value of the land. Worse, we become so separate from it that we harbor illusions of independence from it — we begin to believe that our survival is autonomous from it. The land, the source of our spiritual and social wealth then becomes but a commodity rather than the foundation of our civiliation. Continued apathy toward the decisions now being made regarding the land is expensive, perhaps more expensive than we understand. If the land is the material from which we derive everyhing we do, knowledge about it is the mortar of the future.

My hope for this book is best expressed by an earlier writer, Sir Walter Raleigh in 1600:

"In these pages, as in all I have ever written or propose to write, it is my aim to stimulate, not to satisfy curiosity, and it is no part of my object to save my readers the labor of observation or of thought. For labor is life, and death lives when power lives unused."

It is my hope that this book offers information and inspiration that we might look at the land in a different light, seeing not merely property, but our foundation and our future.

First books are always breach births for authors and there has been a huge circle of friends, colleagues and family who have helped me to pull this one. I would like to extend my thanks and appreciation to all of the people I interviewed for sharing their views and making this book live with the addition of their voices. Space has not permitted all of the interviews conducted to be used, but all of the thoughts offered in the interviews added greatly to my own thinking about public lands. I'd specifically like to thank Hank Deutsch for his help, Rod Nash for guidance and gracious use of his materials, and the rest of the people who agreed to meet me in airports inbetween flights. I'd especially like to thank my editor and good friend, Betsy Armstrong for her humour and golden friendship, and Bob Baron and the rest of the folks at Fulcrum for believeing in a new author. I'd also like to thank Ted Morello for believing in my writing ability a long time ago, despite my fondness for "which-that" sentences. Most importantly, I'd like to thank all of my parents who have been incredibly supportive in every way — so much so that they even feigned interest when I discussed the details of public land history over dinner.

* Willa Cather, *O Pioneers*, (Houghton Mifflin Company, Boston, 1913, 1941)

**Wallace Stegner, "The Wilderness Idea" in *Wilderness: American's Living Heritage*, Ed. David Brower (San Francisco, Sierra Club, 1961)

DEVILS TOWER NATIONAL MONUMENT, WYOMING

CHAPTER 1

THE JUNCTURE

The concept of "public land" is a strange one. How do we begin to comprehend vast parcels of land that are owned by all of us yet which few of us ever see or visit, much less use? In the pursuit of a definition of public lands, perhaps the first thought that comes to mind when visualizing the public lands in the western thirteen states are the national parks and preserves — places like Yellowstone, Yosemite, Canyonlands — which are open for a visit by any one of us, the public, at any time. The idea of public and joint owner-ship of the parks may be easier to understand, if only because of the pride we feel in our national park and refuge system. But the national parks represent only ten percent of our public lands; there are some 600 million other acres of this publicly-owned land in the western states that are outside of the national park system. That is an area three times the present day size of the thirteen original colonies of the United States. Access and use by the public of these other 600 million acres of public land is limited by private lessees or by federal managers, who sit in offices thousands of miles from the land itself. Officially, public lands are those that are held in trust for all of us — a benefit of living in the United States, if you will. Our federal employees — once known as federal servants — manage the lands with the nebulous objective of "the public good" from Washington D.C. and their field offices throughout the country.

*I*n all that section lying
beyond the hundredth meridian on the east, and the Cascade
Range and the Sierra Nevada Mountains on the west, and
within these limits, from the Mexican line on the south to the
international boundary on the north, a totally different set of
conditions, geographical, physical and climactic, are found
to exist. Within this vast area agriculture, as understood and
pursued in the valley of the Mississippi and to the westward,
has no existence . . . it may be safely affirmed that, except in
the immediate valleys of the mountain streams, where by
dint of individual effort water may be diverted for irrigating
purpose, title to the public lands cannot be honestly acquired
under the homestead laws.

General Land Office
Annual Report of the
Commissioner
1875

The question of ownership of these lands is almost as hotly contested as the question of whom should be the primary beneficiary of the wealth within natural resources of these lands. Does that non-existent body of everyone, yet no one in particular that is defined as the "public," own these lands? Or do the lands belong to each of us individually or on a joint-tenant basis? Do the lands belong to the government that manages them or is the government merely in the position of trustee to manage these lands for the people?

From the Washington perspective, these lands are called the "federally-managed lands" or "federal lands," as if the government were a separate entity that was able to own land as you or I might own our backyards. In the ages of kingdoms, when the king did claim ownership to his country's land, such a concept of ownership made sense. Under the system of a government "by and for the people," the concept of "government" ownership begins to resemble something out of *Alice in Wonderland*. Out west, these lands are called the public lands, to be used by the public and owned by each of us, with federal management often considered to be an imposition on our free-will as U.S. citizens. Through an argument that no doubt some people will condemn as being absurdly simple, for the purposes of this book, I am suggesting that the public lands belong to us, the public.

Setting aside the question of ownership for a moment, the fact remains that the public lands are vital to us as a people. They are the source of real wealth that has enabled the United States to be one of the richest countries in the world on scales that have little to do with bank accounts and personal income. Public or private land, the simple bottom line is that it is the land alone that makes this country exist, the land is the national treasury. For what else is there to a country's existence but the land itself? The public's lands — our lands — are what is left in the national accounts, providing the potential and the security for the future.

After we've resolved the concept of ownership of the public lands to our individual satisfaction, then we must ask who is *really* determining the policy that manages our lands. Who has final decision-making power over these lands? The answer to each of

these questions rests in the individual perspective and understanding of the inquisitors, be they rancher, city dweller in the
west or on the east coast, policy maker, or a person living in any
one of the fifty states of the United States who may not have daily,
monthly or even yearly use of the public lands.

Each and every one of us is a special interest group of sorts
when it comes to defining what we want to do with the land that is
being managed for us by the Federal government. Within the
smoke of confusion over the definition of the public lands and the
appointing of a primary beneficiary of the land's wealth, the public
lands have the rare distinction of being all things to all people,
accurately or not. To some, the public lands are those which
should give benefit to the public at large, or to certain members of
the public, whom the public has defined through a patchwork
design of regulations. To others, the concept of public land means
lands that have been locked up from private use and which are
unavailable for the "best use" — the most efficient use of the
resources, the "real" use of the land. Still to others, the public
lands are the national safety deposit box, a place to store the natural
resources for future generations not to be touched by today's
generations. To policy makers, the public's lands present continual
legal conundrums, as the battle is fought out in the blurred
ideological differences in definitions of terms like stewardship,
conservation or preservation. To technical experts in the field, the
concept of public land raises the question of "who's on first"
politically: they must follow today's policy trends based on today's
estimations of highest value or greatest importance. Yet these
policies determine the face of the resource, fifty to a hundred years
into the future, and do not allow for the possible change in the
definition of highest value of our resources in the future.

Regardless of each of our individual interests in the public
lands, the concept of public lands is one that seems to inspire the
heights of argument and controversy among those who feel they
have a stake in the matter. Unfortunately public land arguments
also inspire the depths of boredom to the public at large, as we, as
individuals, wrongly perceive that we do not have a stake in the
outcome of such discussions.

These acres of land are vital to each of us, each in our own way and for our own reasons, whether we live miles away from the public's land or across the fence from it. Had early leaders not attached some value to this unknown land which lay beyond the narrow limits of the colonies precariously perched on its coastal edge, historians note that at least half of the United States as we now know it could be under the rule of another country or under a different form of government.[1]

Despite the ambiguity of the concept of public lands, the lands themselves are real and dynamic. They are the physical source of the materials and natural resources upon which our existence depend. Some would also argue that they are the heart of the American spirit, past, present and future: the high peaks of the Rocky Mountains, the Sierra Nevadas or the Brooks Range in Alaska appear challenging yet intriguing; the range lands reveal a subtle, unique beauty of light and shadow dancing over the broad plains of Wyoming or Nevada. Driving through the land on the nation's highways, looking at the immense Western horizon, you might wonder just who does own all of this land that makes up the vast expanse that is the American West. Chances are, the answer to your question of ownership . . . is you.

Walking through the nation's forests, you might see trees that grew proud and strong when explorers Lewis and Clark pushed the limits of the unknown and wandered their way through the wilderness that was the American West. Pausing on the plains of Montana today, you can see the swell of buttes and plains that looked the same a hundred-plus years ago at the battle of the Little Big Horn. The lands that are the public's lands in the American West reveal the history of this country and yet simultaneously provide the pallet for the present and the future of the United States.

It is a goal of *Lands of Brighter Destiny* that you will not only better understand just what public lands are, but also have a sense of what these lands mean to you as a partial owner of the public lands in the western United States. It is also a goal to acquaint you with the nature of the lands of the west and to take stock of what the treasury holds at this point in the 20th century, for what we have today and how we are using these resources determines to some extent the choices we, as a people, have in the future.

"Public lands is not a field of study," Associate Professor of Public Resources, Sally Fairfax, cautions.[2] "It is a religion." Fair warning, as we consider the answers to some of the questions of ownership, use, beneficiary, and goals for our land and the creation of a decision-making process that we, as a people, cannot afford to ignore.

We are at a unique juncture in time: it is a moment when past policies and past philosophies of land use are being confronted by the present stock of natural resources. Only in this century did we become aware of the fact that we were able to conquer and develop, tame and manage all of what had been wilderness and open lands. Only in this century did it become apparent that open lands and natural areas serve as a means of protecting our sources of natural resources for the future. Only in this century did we become acutely aware that we could, in fact,diminish the land base that we depend upon for our natural resources. We know to some extent what resources we now have within the public lands, but we don't know what the demands of the future will be.

Although there are lessons to be learned in how we arrived at our present position of ownership of the public lands, it is largely water under the policy bridge in planning for the unknown of the future. Although we can try to redress past land philosophies with current policy, that approach does not provide pro-active thought about what we want from the land — from this treasury of natural resources— in the future. Nor does such retroactive policy-making provide the thoughtful approach necessary to meet the needs and goals of the future.

We are at a juncture at which we should take stock of what resources we have and look ahead to meeting the unknown future needs. Land is not something we have been taught to think about unless our employment is reliant upon it. But what could we think about if there were no land, no natural resources and thus no treasury that provides our wealth and the security for our way of life? Public land policy is simply a plan for the present and the future and a way to forge the lifestyle that each of us wants and expects from a country as wealthy as ours. That policy can only be designed to reflect the public's wishes and hopes for the future if

we understand the stock we have at hand now and the choices we
are being required to make.

SOME DEFINITIONS

Imagine for a moment that you are driving west across the
rolling swells of the Great Plains, through Kansas and Nebraska.
The car begins to work a little harder and the gas mileage decreases
markedly as you drive, even though you see that there is no overtly
significant change in the land around you. You have just crossed
the Hundredth Meridian, where the elevation begins to climb from
3,350 feet to the 5000 plus feet above sea level of the Colorado
Plateau. This is where the West begins. In the states west of the
Hundredth Meridian — a sort of border that is imaginary, yet very
real as a physical point of change — the public owns from 28
percent to 89 percent of the land in each of those thirteen states,
compared to only one percent in states like Oklahoma or Massachusetts. Alaska alone contains 45 percent of the total public land
in the United States; the eleven other western states (excluding
Hawaii for now) contain 87 percent of the rest of the public land to
be found in the entire United States.[3]

The thirteen western states, with Alaska and Hawaii included,
contain some 1.1 billion acres of public and private land together:
equal to 49.9 percent of the total U.S. land mass. Sixty percent of
that one billion acres in the west is the public's land, owned by the
people of the United States. It is managed by the federal government, all supposedly to benefit you, the individual citizen. Looked
at in another way, the federal government is managing land in the
west that is equivalent to the size of 128 Massachusetts, or 23.4
Pennsylvanias or 6.7 Californias. It all boils down to each citizen
of the United States having a personal ownership of some 2.92
acres somewhere in the thirteen western states. These acres could
hypothetically be in the middle of U.S. forest land, in the range
lands, in the heart of the wilds of Alaska or in the middle of
Yellowstone National Park. I have left out of this inventory of
western public lands, the lands set aside for Indian reservations
and the lands used by the military.

Map 1 will help you to make sense of where these vast amounts of western land actually sit. In the shaded areas of the states shown are public lands in the west. In Chapter 2, we will take a more detailed look at the lands each of the agencies manage.

To get a better understanding of the overall picture of the public's lands in the west, some of the trends in use and management of your lands can be noted here:

• 68.5 million acres of land ranging from plains and desert to high mountain peaks and tundra have been set aside as national parks in the west. That's only 10 percent of the total acreage managed.

• Alaska alone contains 83 percent of that 10 percent of land in the National Park System. Taking Alaska out of the picture, only 3 percent of the public's western lands have been set aside in the national parks.

• The U.S. Forest Service and the Bureau of Land Management (BLM) essentially split management of the bulk of the public's lands, with the BLM managing some 340.6 million acres. That's about the size of the original thirteen colonies. A third of that 340.6 million acres is in Alaska.

• 15 percent of Forest Service land has been designated as part of the National Wilderness Preservation System. A quarter of that wilderness is in Alaska.[4]

• 7 percent of BLM land is in Wilderness Study classification. But .003 percent of it has actually been set aside as wilderness thus far.[5]

• 60 percent of western low sulfur coal is located in the public's lands, as are 35 percent of the nation's uranium reserves.[6]

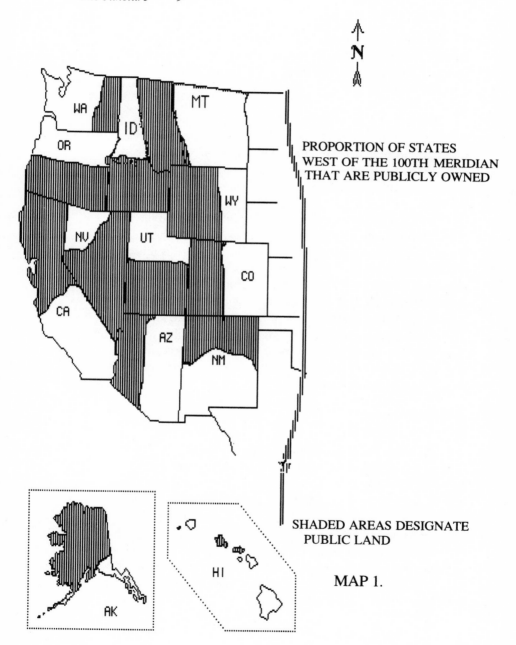

N

PROPORTION OF STATES
WEST OF THE 100TH MERIDIAN
THAT ARE PUBLICLY OWNED

SHADED AREAS DESIGNATE
PUBLIC LAND

MAP 1.

• There is no federal inventory of minerals or oil and gas on the public lands; all information comes from private companies seeking to develop the resources. [see Chapter 2 for more information.]

The actual numbers that describe the public's land are about the only point of agreement between the various vocal factions who participate in determining public land policy. The present uses for the land, how it is used, and in some views misused, is the fuel for the on-going debate regarding public land policy in the West.

This is a debate that has seemed to intensify with the knowledge that even the vast amount of land available to the United States for public domain does have limits. As large as this country is, there is no more land to conquer or explore, no veil of the unknown to provide the basis for believing in the existence of perpetual abundance. Unlike 125 years ago, the boundaries of the public's lands and the extent of the resources are known. They are no longer obscured by an incomprehensible treasure of resources that was heightened by an aura of wildness and mystery that whetted our national appetites when settlers first arrived on the American continent.

SOME HISTORY

An overview of the 200 year history of public-land philosophy and policy in the United States is dominated by the foresight of really only two men: Thomas Jefferson and Theodore Roosevelt. In our present time, Morris Udall and William O. Douglas have provided and acted upon a similar caliber of philosophy and vision regarding public-land policy. Although there were other significant participants in the process, the inspiration and encouragement to place a sense of importance on the use of natural resources and actual thought about land policy emanated mostly from these men.

"The work we are now doing is, I trust, done for posterity, in such a way they don't but need to repeat it. We shall delineate with correctness the great arteries of this country; those who come after us will extend the same features as they become acquainted of them and fill up the canvas we begin."

Thomas Jefferson 1803 [7]

This history of the acquisition of the public's land is surrounded by the golden aura of Manifest Destiny: of God's Chosen People filling up the bountiful land of America from sea to shining sea and bringing the experiment of democracy into fruition; of pioneers who risked their lives to settle America, seemingly more out of altruism than personal gain, if one is to believe the personal histories of their journey west. Personal economic gain, however, had a lot to do with the interest in acquiring and in dispensing the new and untamed land that was full of treasures for the people of the new United States, whether for natural resources or for a better quality of living for anyone who reached for it.[8]

"Remember that of the passengers on the Mayflower, two-thirds were investors in the trip and one-third were religious freedom-seekers," notes Professor Fairfax. "I think the same can be said for those who ventured west: two-thirds, economic interest and one-third, freedom seeking."[9]

The first investment into the business of public land management for the United States came in 1803 with the Louisiana Purchase. In one stroke of the pen, Jefferson almost doubled the size of the United States and took a giant step into the unknown. The country had acquired some 100 acres per person with the purchase, at a cost of 15 million dollars. It was only three cents per acre, but still 9 million dollars more than the new country had in the treasury.[10] One need only imagine today what our reactions would be if the President of the United States announced that he had purchased some 530 million acres of inaccessible wilderness, about which very little if anything was known, with the limited financial resources of a finite treasury and without consulting Congress — and then had the nerve to say that he did it for the benefit of the people of the United States. Jefferson defended his gamble for the future in this way:

"The Executive, in seizing the fugitive occurrence which so advances the good of their country, have done an act beyond the Constitution. The Legislature, in casting behind them the metaphysical subtleties and risking themselves like faithful servants, must ratify and pay for it, and throw themselves on their country for doing for them unauthorized what we know they would have done for themselves had they been in a situation to do it. It is the case of a guardian, investing the money of his ward in purchasing an important adjacent territory, and saying to him when of age, I did this for your good; I pretend to no right to bind you: you may disavow me, and I must get out of the scrape as I can: I thought it my duty to risk myself for you. But we shall not be disavowed by the nation, and their act of ind-emnity will confirm and not weaken the Constitution, by more strongly marking out its lines."[11]

Members of the public angrily responded to Jefferson's going into the land business: "We are to give money of which we have too little for land of which we already have too much."[12] Given that land at the time had no outwardly obvious value, except in the visible natural resources or in the sheer quantity itself, I suspect our reactions today might be the same.

Yet, there is something captivating about the vision of Thomas Jefferson seeing the necessity of the Louisiana Purchase as a tool by which to fortify and confirm the destiny of his grand experiment in Democracy. Equally, the subsequent tale of Lewis and Clark's venture across the great unknown — a land that was then still only imagination and dream until they crossed the vast acres and beheld the Pacific Ocean — helped to set a fire for the rest of the land acquisition that would garner for the United States its present size of 2.3 billion acres within 100 years of its founding. This vision, which defined land holdings as the foundation for greatness in the United States, also set the tone for future thought toward land as a tangible asset, benefiting not just the private owner, but the public at large. It became a lust for land in which land was defined not only as power and security, but as wealth and as a direction for the future. Historian Bernard DeVoto described the purchase in these terms in his introduction to the *Journals of Lewis and Clark:*[13]

"The Louisiana Purchase was one of the most important events in world history. It was an event of such magnitude that, as Henry Adams said, its results are beyond measurement. Not only did it double the area of the United States, not only did it add to our wealth resources of incalculable value, not only did it provide a potential that was certain to make us a great power, not only did it make equally certain that we would expand beyond the Rockies to the Pacific, and not only did it secure us against foreign victory on any scale conceivable in the nineteenth century — it also provided the centripetal, unifying force that would hold the nation firm against disruptive forces from within. Whether or not the rebellion that became the Civil War was inevitable, the Purchase had made certain that it could not succeed. And there is no aspect of our national life, no part of our social and political structure, and no subsequent event in the main course of our history that it has not affected."

Abraham Lincoln expressed the essence of this new American attitude toward land in his Second Annual Message in 1862:

"A nation may be said to consist of its territory, its people and its laws. The territory is the only part which is of certain durability. One generation passeth away and another generation cometh, but the earth abideth forever. It is of the first importance to duly consider and estimate this ever-enduring part. That portion of the earth's surface which is owned and inhabited by the people of the United States is well adapted to be the home of one national family, and it is not well adapted for two or more. Its vast extent and its variety of climate and productions are of advantage in

*this age for one people, whatever they might have been in
former ages."14*

In the space of sixty-five years from Jefferson's 1803 purchase of the Louisiana territory, the country tripled its size and
had already begun to dispose of the land to the beneficiaries: the
public. Map 2 highlights the land acquisitions of U.S growth
into the "lands of brighter destiny," as the lands were called at
the time. Remember that all of the eleven western states and
Alaska were essentially part of the public domain — *i.e.* belonging to the public — at one time. The only exceptions were those
areas that were already privately owned when the cessions took
place with Mexico or Spain. The map, provided by the Bureau of
Land Management in their Public Lands Annual, explains when
and what was acquired.

With the borders secured, the debate then began regarding
the value of the land itself. Was value to be measured by the standards of the time in the 1860s and 1870s, or was value to be
estimated, based on the future purpose of the land?

"It is safe to say that the prosperity of our people depends
directly on the energy and intelligence with which our natural
resources are used," argued President Theodore Roosevelt in
1909 in his opening address to governors at a conference on
conservation. "It is equally clear that those resources are the final
basis of national power and perpetuity. Finally, it is ominously
evident that those resources are in the course of rapid
exhaustion."15

Few have argued with Roosevelt's definition of value of the
land and the natural resources, even today. His last sentence,
however, sounded the call to a battle which still thrives today:
whether the resources are running out. His comments also
identify the seeds of what would become an entire philosophy
toward public land policy in the United States that equally thrives
almost 80 years later in the camps of some public policy factions.

In the years between 1867, when the entire west was public
domain and 79 percent of the entire United States lay in public
hands, and 1984, the government has dispensed some 1.14

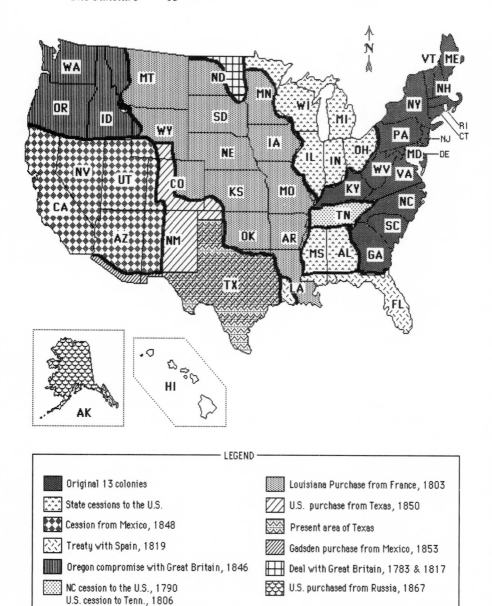

Map 2. Land Acquisitions, 1776 Forward.

billion acres of land into private and state hands. More specifically, in the west, out of that 79 percent, 12 western states were created, along with 19 others outside the west.[16] The railroads were granted 61.1 million acres of land in the western states other than in Alaska and Hawaii, under the common belief that the land would increase in value if people could get to it more easily than having to face the arduous overland wagon routes.[17]

Today, 60 percent of the land in the western 13 states is managed by the federal government. Alaska and Nevada are still more than 80 percent public land. The manner in which the rest of the public's lands were dispensed is still a point of contention among some involved in public land policy. Much of the land was sold to increase the treasury of a country that was not yet taxing its citizens. Some would say that the land was sold to bring revenues into a dwindling treasury; others would call it a give-away at any price. Through a push by Horace Greeley[18] and the subsequent Home-- stead Acts that are discussed in Chapter 2, public domain became available to the public in large chunks for a nominal fee.[19]

There are entire books devoted to the history of the public lands — both acquisition and disposal — covering the subject in far more detail than is necessary here, to understand what we have in the stock of the public's land in the west today.[20] What is necessary is enough history simply to provide a sense of the debates and the foundation for the questions facing us — so that we can look forward and ask what we should do with the lands that are still ours today. A forward thinking policy does not attempt to redress past affronts — perceived or real — made by past public land policies and philosophies held in a certain time. Rather, we must take a fresh step forward to look at the potential demands of the future.

The first area to capture the imagination — and thus the legal preservation by the government — was Yellowstone in 1872. Although by 1872, the limits of the country were known physically, large portions of the interior of the west were still unmapped and less known. Yellowstone must have seemed mystical to those few who ventured upon it. While the rest of the country was taken with the pioneer spirit and impulse to conquer the land, Yellowstone became a source of material for fantasy for the imagination. Yet, it was real, and fantastic enough to represent adventure and such beauty that early reports were called lies. Only an 85-hour ride by the newly completed Northern Pacific Railroad from New York, an early writer described the nation's first experiment in preservation as "the most dazzlingly beautiful sight I ever beheld."[21] A first report of the Yellowstone was written by Bayard Taylor in 1873, who drew from exploration reports by U.S. Geological Survey teams and a series of articles in Scribner's to acquaint the public with its new national treasure:

"It is the wildness, the grandeur of the enclosing mountain scenery, and still more the curious, beautiful, wonderful and stupendous natural phenomena which characterize the region, that have raised it to sudden fame and cause it to be set apart by our national government as a grand national play-ground and museum of unparalleled, indeed incomparable, marvels, free to all men for all time."[22]

The Forest Preservation Act of 1891, which allowed the president to set aside public domain in a forest reserve, was passed when there was fear that the country would be running out of timber if some forests weren't set aside.[23] We'll see more about these individual steps toward some semblance of land policy in each of the sections in Chapter 2. By 1897, some 40 million acres of forest had been removed from the public domain, by various presidents, even though there was no provision in the laws to manage the set-aside lands. President Theodore Roosevelt brought the western forest reserves up to the present-day size even as he paved the way for conservation as a trend in public land policy.[24]

"What right has any citizen of a free country, whatever his foresight and shrewdness, to seize on sources of life for his own behalf that are the common heritage of all; what right has legislation or court to help in the seizure; and striking still more

The American earth represents our greatest heritage. The right to pure water streams, virgin forests, the woodchuck and the antelope, and the other exciting wonders of the woods are as basic to our freedom as the special rights enshrined in our Bill of Rights. Granite rocks are to me the sturdy character of Samuel Adams who wrote moving tracts on our Revolution.They are also the unbending will of the men of Concord and Lexington. Men do reflect their environment. It molds their character — whether it be the sea, the desert, or the mountain.

William O. Douglas
"Wilderness and Human Rights"
1961

*deeply, what right has any generation to wholly consume, much
less to waste, those sources of life without which the children or
the children's children must freeze?"*

asked W.J. McGee, who would soon become the assistant to
Gifford Pinchot in the Theodore Roosevelt Administration in
1907.[25] Between 1909 and 1934, minerals were removed from
the public access for the Naval Reserves. Then, in 1934, the
Taylor Grazing Act ended homesteading in the lower 48 states,
giving administration of the newly designated grazing lands to
the Grazing Service, soon to be known as the Bureau of Land
Management.

By the 1940s, the public lands had become much as they
are today. With the quantities, and to a large extent, the qualities
of the land known, only the tenor of land management of the
lands remained unknown. The arguments over the management
of the public lands took off with the same spirit that homesteaders took to the settling of the land in the previous century.
Some trends in managing the resources of the public lands have
changed with the passing trends of the last 55 years, while others
date back one hundred years and bring us to the arguments over
the management of your land today.

Management policies for our lands and resources have been
a hundred years in the making, yet always without an overall
goal or objective. With few notable exceptions, a general public
land philosophy over these hundred years has been piecemeal
rather than thoughtfully considered and has been only as forward
thinking as the term of a presidential administration. Surely we
can do better than a patchwork philosophy of land management
for our resources which have lasted a millennium and which
must, out of basic necessity, last another.

Some factions of the public policy debate over the land
argue that the public's land should be preserved for an undetermined future generation to use. Some camps argue simply
that the lands should be preserved for perpetuity, while others
argue that all lands should be available for multiple use now and
in the future. Others seem to think that the lands would be both

better preserved and/or used more efficiently if the federal government got out of the land management business altogether and let
private individual-owners or non-profit private boards take over
the decision of how best to apportion and manage the natural resources of the public lands. Some westerners resent the federal
government still managing a majority of the western land — a
feeling similar to that which the original thirteen colonies voiced
regarding foreign rule. Others see the lands as being locked up,
belonging to the federal government and being managed in the
same ambiguous way "the Feds" have managed them for fifty
years. Specifics of these arguments, as well as other voices
speaking to other notions on public land management can be
found in Chapter 3, The Visions.

Somewhere in all of these options, and in the multitude of
variations and combinations that stem from them, each of us
might find a voice which reflects our own feelings toward our
2.92 acres or toward the whole 661.882 million acres of public
land in the west. A policy of land use is sort of a vision —
individually or on a national scale. To rely only upon the voices
of "experts" or policy-makers to create such a vision is to ab-
rogate our individual right to participate in our future. By being
apathetic toward the use of our land, we mute our own voices
and eliminate our right to choose a direction and a philosophy for
use of the very thing which sustains our society and us individually. We often hear the term "vital interest" used by our
representatives in Washington, D.C., but rarely is it associated
with the management and use of our lands, our natural resources, which are the basic foundation of our wealth as a
country and are the only source of material for our future.

Some questions we might be asking ourselves will help to
formulate a policy direction for the public's land — for our land.
Our continued silence will only create a land with no policy, or
worse, policy by default because we are not interested in
participating in a vision of our future or the planning philosophy
for the resources to meet those future needs. Like not planning
our personal income to see us through next year, not considering
what we simply want from the future — and thus need from the

land that supports those hopes and dreams — is to be foolhardy.
The primary question among these may be the hardest to answer,
but it is a question that is the foundation of the rest of this exploration into the public lands; it is equally a question that is so
very important at this juncture of planning in public land policy:
What is the value of the public's lands of the west to you, as an
individual? What is the value of the lands to you as a member of
the public?

To put it in more simple, personal terms, what do you want
from these lands we share? What do you expect to gain? How do
they enhance your life?

• Do you expect to see them in the future? Knowing the limits of
the stock of the resources of the public's land, what should be
used now and what should be left for the future?

In writing this book, each of the people interviewed in
Chapter 3 were asked these last two questions and I now pose
them to you:

• Look a hundred years into the future, what is the view you
would like to have of the vast acreage that you in part own: the
national parks, the forests, the wide grasslands, the wilderness
and the desert?

• From that point one hundred years forward, look back at our
generation and at what we are doing today. How would you
assess our land use policies, as historians might? What would
you change?

The answers to such questions are not easy, but they are the
beginnings of policy and vision. They are the seed of planning
and foresight that is true to the democratic ideal of a voice joining
with a vision to determine the course of our future. The answers
to the above questions won't come as much from the facts you
read as from inside you, from your perceptions of the value of
the public lands and resources and your vision for the future.

THE GORE RANGE, EAGLES NEST WILDERNESS, COLORADO

CHAPTER 2

THE STOCK

Now let's take a closer, more detailed look at some of the public land in the West. It may seem incongruent to try to describe land with numbers, for the picture each of us holds of these lands is probably based on intangible perceptions of what we gain from the land as a whole. The wealth of natural resources remains our primary source of richness in this country; the factor that set apart the United States from other wealthy western nations in tangible and intangible ways.

Yet, the Federal Government, as managing agent, tends to see the western public lands in terms of statistics, numbers and otherwise basically undistinguishable ways. A large part of the management policy is based on the neutral and even sterile ways of quantifying and describing the land— a forest measured in board feet rather than looked at as having with certain characteristics involving slope, growing conditions, habitat, weather.

What follows is a rough sketch of the public lands in the West, divided by agency management or quality of land: the Forest Service, the Bureau of Land Management, the National Park Service, in which I've included wildlife refuges and wilderness areas, and finally, Alaska, which represents a separate case unto itself. By better understanding what we have in our natural resource treasury, we can better understand the issues facing the use and the future purpose of our lands.

ARAPAHOE NATIONAL FOREST, COLORADO

I. THE FOREST SERVICE
Part of the U.S. Department of Agriculture

"The President . . . may, from time to time, set apart and reserve, in any State of territory having public land bearing forests, in any part of the public lands wholly or in part covered with timber of undergrowth: whether of commercial value or not; as public reservations, and the President shall; by proclamation, declare the establishment of such reservations and limits thereof."

26 Stat. 1103; 16 USC 471

Section 24 of the above statute established the Forest Service system in 1891 under the provisions of the Withdrawal Act. In 1897, the Organic Act further delineated the role of the Forest Service to set aside the nation's forests for use in the future.

Together the forests in the West comprise 254 thousand square miles of forest and grasslands. If all of the national forests in the western thirteen states were put together, they would equal an area just under the size of Texas. The lands of the Forest Service are managed with an annual budget of 1.952 billion dollars — basically twelve dollars per acre. Nineteen percent of the land in the National Forest System has been designated as wilderness — "to protect watersheds and wildlife habitat, preserve scenic and historic resources, and promote scientific research, primitive recreation, solitude, physical and mental challenge, and inspiration for the

benefit of all of the American people," as many of the state
wilderness bills read. Yet 95 percent of all the wilderness in the
U.S. is in the western thirteen states, with eighteen percent of
that designated wilderness in Alaska.

The rest of the forest lands that are not part of the wilderness
system or are not being considered or studied for wilderness designation are known as "multiple use" lands, open to timbering,
oil, gas, coal and mineral production and grazing. They are the
lands that provide the natural resources of our society. All of the
lands — wilderness and multiple use lands alike — are open to
the unlikely partners of mineral exploration and recreation. The
Forest Service, however, does not manage the sub-surface resources, the Bureau of Land Management (BLM) (a wing of the
Department of Interior) does. The Forest Service's responsibility is to "protect and manage the affected surface resources,"
providing environmental impact statements on the proposed energy or mineral development under the nation's forests. In 1983,
just under 21,000 mineral leases were approved, 4,000 more
than were called for by Congress in the performance goal of the
Forest Service, and 2,000 more than were planned. The Forest
Service says it did not process the 2,000 energy leases that were
applied for in wilderness study areas, according to Congress's
directive. Some 4,400 energy lease applications were received
that year.

There is much discussion in the early 1980's over proposed
land exchanges between the Forest Service and the Bureau of
Land Management. The measure, the agencies indicate, is a
housekeeping move, to put more of the nation's forests into the
hands of the foresters. Such exchanges in the years to come
would designate the surface manager to be the responsible
agency for the below ground minerals as well as the timber.

These are the basics of the structure of the Forest Service lands.
The meat, if you will, is the character and the controversy that
has surrounded the National Forest System almost from its
inception.

SOME HISTORY

As with the history of legislation of the rest of the public lands (with the possible exception of the national park system); the laws structuring the nation's forests and their use were sort of an afterthought — a response to what law-makers saw as an impending crisis. They thought the country was running out of timber in the late 1890's and something had to be done to stop the free cutting and timbering that was taking place.[1] Even Section 24 of the statutes setting up the Forest Preserve system was an afterthought, tacked on to an act, that had among its other objectives, a measure to ease the burden of trespassers on government timber land and another measure to repeal the Timber Culture Act of 1873.[2] Section 24 gave the President discretion to withdraw lands from the public domain as forest reservations, without Congressional approval. The power given the Executive branch wasn't limited until 1907, when the General Withdrawal Act forbade further increase of the national forests in six western states.

The general terms of Section 24 helped to set the tone for some of today's questions surrounding Forest Service management and the agency's primary role of responsibility and objective in caring for the nation's forests. Neither the Organic Act nor the Withdrawal Act precisely defined the criteria for setting aside the forest preserves; nor was the purpose defined for such forest preserves as to how the resources were to be used, when and for what purposes. It was a case of everyone seeing in the law the individual reasons they wanted to set aside forest land, be it watershed protection, timbering or preservation of wilderness.

One of the first values attributed to preserving forests in the United States was wood for the Navy. Congress in 1799 authorized purchase of timber lands for the Navy, legislation that was reaffirmed in 1817 and again in 1827. By 1872, a bill was introduced to manage the forests of the public domain, but failed.

In 1874, President Grant submitted to Congress a message regarding the "cultivation of timber and the preservation of forests." Written by Franklin J. Hough and George B. Emerson of the American Association for the Advancement of Sciences, the message noted that "the time is not too distant when great public injury must result" from the "rapid exhaustion that is taking place" of the forests. "Besides the economical value of timber for construction, fuel and the arts, which is obvious without suggestion," Hough and Emerson wrote, "there are questions of climate that appear to have a close relation to the presence or absence of woodland shade. The drying up of rivulets which feed our mill-streams and navigable rivers and supply our canals, the failure of the sources which supply our cities with pure water, and the growing tendency to floods and drought, resulting from the unequal distribution of the rain-fall since the cutting off of our forests, are subjects of common observation."[3]

The General Land Office took up the call for "withdrawal and reservation regulation of timber sales, preservation and protection" through the years of discussion that followed. The United States started looking to the European continent for results of their experience in dealing with their forests. Yet, through all of this discussion, no real tenor was set that designated an explicit, real objective for use of the forests of the public lands. In 1882 Franklin Hough, by this time Secretary of Agriculture, published his third and final paper that recommended that the "principal bodies of timber land still remaining the property of the government be withdrawn from sale or grant under the existing modes for conveying the public lands and that they be placed under regulations calculated to secure an economical use of the existing timber . . . and the young timber, in all leases for cutting, being reserved and protected for a future supply."

In 1881, President Benjamin Harrison proclaimed the first forest reserve — the Yellowstone Forest Reserve in Wyoming, adjacent to the then newly established Yellowstone National Park, which had been set aside in 1872 as a natural wonder. The forest today remains wild enough to provide habitat for the grizzly bear. From Harrison's proclamation foreword, the forests were reserved for "the public good" although still without specific definition of just how that public good was to be best served.

The American Forestry Association in 1889 petitioned Congress to withdraw the public timberlands from sale and to appoint a commission to make recommendations for management, noting that:

"First, they are valuable parts of the property of the nation . . Second, they will be needed as an important source of timber supply for the Western States for all time to come. If the population of this country is to continue what it is now, to say nothing of its probable great increase, these forests must always be looked to to supply the people of a vast region with timber for buildings, railroads, mining, and many manufacturing industries . . .and third, the greatest value of these forests to the present and future inhabitants of the Western states is in the assistance they render to agriculture through their influence on the water supply and the climate."

It was amazing that the American Forestry Association was predicting and describing the conflict in forestry management the West faces today and over the coming years when the Associaion said in the same report that:

"No system of reservoirs, even the most costly and ingenious, can take the place of the forests on any large scale. The most that it can do is to co-operate with them. It is respectfully suggested that the true value and use of these mountain forests has never been properly considered by this Government. It has apparently never realized that mountain forest land differs from all other land in this important respect, that its condition can not substantially be changed without disastrous results; that it must, for the sake of the properly (sic) agricultural land, always remain in forest."

Throughout the late 1890's, the sparks of another later battle well known to us today were beginning to glow. Was the purpose of the forest preserves to preserve the forests, maintaining an area "forever wild" or were the forests to be open to multiple use and available for widespread timbering?

By 1896, 16 forests had been designated by presidential proclamation, but there was still no clear forest policy. Nobody
really knew what to do with these forest preserves, except to
keep the public from timbering them. The commission of the
General Land Office, which included Gifford Pinchot, a young
forestry zealot, recommended the creation of thirteen additional
forest reserves in the western states. Congress had had enough
of this unilateral action, with the representatives in the western
states complaining the loudest about the presidential proclama-
tions and the amount of land being set aside without their participation. On May 1, 1897, the commission submitted its final
report, recommending "a system of general forest management
for the nation," which would lead to the Organic Act of 1897,
which defined the purposes for management of the preserves,
and established the Forest Service. Section 2 of the Act is the
most often quoted:

*"That no public forest reservations shall be established except to im-
prove and protect the forest within the reservation or for the purpose of
securing favorable conditions of water flow and to insure a continuous
supply of timber for the people of the States wherein such forest reservations are located; but it is not the purpose of this act to authorize the
inclusion within such forest reservations land more valuable for the
mineral thereon or for agricultural purposes than for timber . . ."*

The debate that led to the creation or the Organic Act, however,
was not so unilateral in the objectives of the use of the forest reservations. Instead, the debate forecast the kinds of issues we face
today in defining the best use of the national forests. Representative Thomas C. McRae of Arkansas argued that the object of the
reservation was to protect the forest from destruction by "fire and
axe, without excluding the use of these reservations for other purposes. They are not parks set aside for nonuse, but have been
established for economic reasons."

Representative John C. Bell, Colorado, saw the purpose of
the forest preserves a little differently. His view, I think, is
reflective of the different perspective that represents the lands of
the west; his views seem to be born of an arid west:

"It was never the object to establish forest reservations to preserve timber for commercial use. That was foreign to the object: and in my district on three of the reservations established by President Harrison's proclamation; there is scarcely a piece of commercial timber that can be obtained from any of those reservations. The object was not to reserve timber for commercial purposes. The lines were not run with such a purpose in view. The object was to go to the head waters of the White River, to go to the head waters of other great streams and there lay off a plat of timber where the snow fell to a great depth and to provide that timber should not be molested there, not because we wanted to save it for future commercial purposes, but that we wanted to save it for the purpose of conserving the water supply of these rivers for the use of the valleys below . . . That is the reason why the Battle Mountain reservation was set apart. The purpose was to increase the flow of the White River. President Harrison's agents were sent to the Grand Mesa, nine or ten thousand feet above the sea level, to set apart a reserve of timber, not for the timber, but that it might retard the snow melting. Now, it cost probably $25 to get a tree off that mesa. We could not use the timber that grows there if we wanted to, because it would cost so much. The object of making the reserve was to preserve the snow, so as to fill the lakes on that great mesa for the purpose of increasing the flow of the streams for agricultural purposes . . . They are reservations to promote the water supply to the farms in the valleys below."

Another question we will look at in discussing the issues facing the Forest Service today was also considered during the debate of the Organic Act in 1897: the tenor or quality of management of the forest reserves that the country was going to undertake. Is forest management, *per se,* to clearcut sections — taking both tall timber and shrub — to create new growth all of the same age? Or is management culling forests for the tallest trees, leaving the rest of the forest to become the cull stock five, ten, twenty years down the line — a method of forestry cutting known as "selective cutting?" In 1897, this was one view of the issue, brought into the debate on the purposes of management of the newly created Forest Service by Representative Eugene F. Loud of California:

"The trouble is, Mr. Speaker, that some gentlemen misunderstand the object of setting aside a forest reserve. There is a class of technical gentlemen in this country who favor timber culture, and they confound

*timber culture with forest reservation . . . The only object of the forest
reserves in the state of California is to retain the snows upon the
mountains, so that the snows and rains shall not bring down all at once
the full flood upon our valleys, where irrigation is carried on to a great
extent and where it is a necessity, as it is for the production of the crops
of the great San Joaquin Valley. That is the main object of the forest
reserve in the State of California, and not to encourage the growth of
straight trees and clean forests. The more fully you keep the forest in its
natural condition, with a large amount of undergrowth and decayed timber, the more effectually do you attain the object of keeping the snows
upon the mountains. I know that to gentlemen who confound timber
culture with forest reservation, the provision [a provision allowing timbering within the reserve] in this bill appears perfectly harmless, but I
believe and it is the general consensus of men who have investigated
this quesion, that the moment you open the forest reservations to the
cutting of timber you begin to destroy the forest reservations themselves. There is a provision permitting the cutting of timber for mining
purposes, which if carried into effect, will destroy, as I have said, the
forest reservations on the western side of the Sierra Nevada Mountains,
as it has destroyed and denuded the forests on the eastern side."*

After the 1887 laws, as part of one of the provisions of the
Organic Act, the U.S. Geological Service for the first time took
inventory of the forest reserves that existed in the western states
as well as those reserves that might be created into reservations.
The survey took note of fire damage and grazing alike and noted
the use of areas by recreation, mining and local lumbering. By
1905, 85 national forests had been set up in the western 13 states
for a total of 79.37 million acres — almost 49 percent of the total
amount of forest that exists today. There have been, however, a
lot of changes in location and in the size of the specific forests.
The Lewis and Clark forest preserve, for example, that was set
aside in Montana in 1897 decreased in size by a factor of three,
according to today's acreage.

Another important event that was to affect the character of the
Forest Service took place in 1905: the administration of the forest
reserves was transferred to the Department of Agriculture's Bureau of Forestry from the Department of Interior. Pinchot himself
had recommended the transfer in 1898 from the General Land
Office because "it (the Bureau of Forestry) is the only Govern-

ment agency directly related to the vast interests of the private
forest land in the United States. How great these interests are
will appear when it is known that the forest included in farms
alone covers more than 200 million acres — more than four
times the area of all of the forest reserves of the government."
Along with the transfer came a letter from Secretary of Agriculture James Wilson, to Pinchot directing him how to manage
the new forest reserves. The letter sets out the objectives that
have been as controversial to some as they are doctrinaire to
others, and the objectives affected the style of management of the
forests over the last century. Pinchot claimed to have written the
letter himself.

It is interesting to note that not law but one individual's style
of management has served as the philosophy of use and purpose
of the nation's forests for the last one hundred years.

*"In the administration of the forest reserves it must be clearly borne in
mind that all land is to be devoted to its most productive use for the
permanent good of the whole people, and not for the temporary benefit
of individuals of companies. All the resources of the forest reserves are
for use, and this use must be brought about in a thoroughly prompt and
businesslike manner, under such restrictions only as will insure the per-
manence of these resources . . . You will see to it that the water, wood,
and forage of the reserves are conserved and wisely used for the benefit
of the home builder first of all, upon whom depends the best permanent
use of lands and resources alike. The continued prosperity of the agricultural, lumbering, mining and livestock interests is directly dependent
upon a permanent and accessible supply of water, wood, and forage, as
well as upon the present and future use of these resources under bus-
iness-like regulations, enforced with promptness, effectiveness, and
common sense. In the management of each reserve local questions will
be decided upon local grounds; the dominant industry will be considered
first, but with as little restriction to minor industries as may be possible, sudden changes in industrial conditions will be avoided by gradual
adjustment after due notice, and where conflicting interest must be recon-
ciled the question will always be decided from the standpoint of the
greatest good of the greatest number in the long run."[4]*

In 1905, Pinchot changed the names of the preserves to national
forests. President Theodore Roosevelt added a million acres in

1907 by proclamation, getting around legislation Congress had passed (but which the president had not yet signed) forbidding any further creation or enlargement of national forests except by Act of Congress in the states of Washington, Oregon, Montana, Idaho, Wyoming and Colorado. In order to add 16 million more acres to the National Forest System, Roosevelt sent Pinchot out to pick the areas, received Pinchot's recommendation, and signed it into proclamation. Only then did Roosevelt sign the Congressional legislation, that had been sitting on his desk, within the required time. Over the previous seven years, the area within the national forest system had been tripled nationwide with the addition of some 150 million acres. With the Weeks Forest Purchase Act in 1911, the forests of the national system had been essentially set aside; the Weeks Act enabled purchase of national forest land in the eastern states.

Roosevelt's midnight proclamation of the forests in 1907 had secured the national forest system in the states west of the Hundredth Meridian. Theodore Roosevelt had effected more public land policy than any previous 19th century president: if not in the sheer number of acres set aside for "conservation" then in creating a philosophy of conservation of public lands for the public through the National Forest system, by passage of the Antiquities Act of 1906. The Act enables presidents to unilaterally set aside national monuments and establish wildlife reserves and bird sanctuaries.

"The lesson of deforestation in China," Roosevelt said, defending his setting aside of the forests, "is a lesson which mankind should have learned many times already from what has occurred in other places. Denudation leaves naked soil, then gullying cuts down to bare rock; and meanwhile the rock waste buries the bottom lands. When the soil is gone, men must go, and the process does not take long . . ."[5]

*T*he duty of man to man, on which
*the integrity of nations must rest, is no higher than the duty of each
generation to the next; and the obligation of the nation to each actual
citizen is no more sacred than the obligation to the citizen to be, who,
in turn, must bear the nation's duties and responsibilities.*

*In this country, blessed with natural resources in unsurpassed pro-
fusion, the sense of responsibility to the future has been slow to
awaken. Beginning without appreciation of the measure or the value of
natural resources other than land with water for commercial uses, our
forefathers pushed into the wilderness and, through a spirit of enterprise
which is the glory of the nation, developed other great resources. Forests were cleared away as obstacles to the use of the land; iron and coal
were discovered and developed, though for years their presence added
nothing to the price of the land, and through the use of native woods
and metals and fuels, manufacturing grew beyond all precedent, and the
country became a power among the nations of the world.*

*Gradually the timber growing on the ground and the iron and coal
within the ground came to have a market value and were bought and
sold as sources of wealth. Meanwhile, vast holdings of these resources
were acquired by those of greater foresight than their neighbors before
it was generally realized that they possessed value in themselves; and in
this way large interests, assuming monopolistic proportions, grew*

up, with greater enrichment to their holders than the world had seen before, and with the motive of immediate profit, with no concern for the future or thought of the permanent benefit of country and people, a wasteful and profligate use of the resources began and has continued.

The waters, at first recognized only as aids to commerce in supplying transportation routes, were largely neglected. In time this neglect began to be noticed, and along with it the destruction and approaching exhaustion of the forests. This, in turn, directed attention to the rapid depletion of the coal and iron deposits and the misuse of the land.

The public conscience became awakened. Seeing the increased value and noting the destructive consumption and waste of the natural resources, men began to realize that the permanent welfare of the country as well as the prosperity of their offspring were at stake. The wastes which most urgently require checking vary widely in character and amount. The most reprehensible waste is that of destruction, as in forest fires, uncontrolled flow of gas and oil, soil wash, and abandonment of coal in the mines. This is attributable, for the most part, to ignorance, indifference, or false notions of economy, to rectify which is the business of the people collectively.

Nearly as reprehensible is the waste arising from misuse, as in the consumption of fuel in furnaces and engines of low efficiency, the loss of water in floods, the employment of ill-adapted structural materials, the growing of ill-chosen crops, and the perpetuation of inferior stocks of plants and animals, all of which may be remedied. Reprehensible in less degree is the waste arising from nonuse. Since the utilization of any one resource is necessarily progressive and dependent on social and industrial conditions and the concurrent development of other resources, nonuse is sometimes unavoidable. It becomes reprehensible when it affects the common welfare and entails future injury. Then, it should be rectified in the general interest.

For the prevention of waste the most effective means will be found in the increase and diffusion of knowledge, from which is sure to result an aroused public sentiment demanding prevention. The people have the matter in their own hands. They may prevent or limit the destruction of resources and restrain misuse through the enactment and enforcement of appropriate state and federal laws.

At every stage in the growth of our country, strong men grew stronger through the exercise of nations building and their intelligence and patriotism grew with their strength. The spirit and vigor of our people are the chief glory of the republic. Yet even as we have neglected our natural resources, so have we been thoughtless of life and health. Too long have we overlooked that grandest of our resources, human life. Natural resources are of no avail without men and women to develop them, and only a strong and sound citizenship can make a nation permanently great.We can not too soon enter on the duty of conserving our chief source of strength by the prevention of disease and the prolongation of life. Wastes reduced and resources saved are the first but not the last objective of conservation. The material resources have an additional value when their preservation adds to the beauty and habitability of the land. Ours is a pleasant land in which to dwell. To increase its beauty and augment its fitness can not but multiply our pleasure in it and strengthen the bonds of our attachment.

Theodore Roosevelt
The National Conservation
Commission Report
1909

POST-WORLD WAR II —
CULTIVATING THE GARDEN

"The national forests are designed by Congress for 'multiple use.' That is the professed policy. I had long suspected that 'multiple' use was semantics for making cattlemen, sheepmen, lumbermen, miners the main beneficiaries. After they gutted and razed the forests, then the rest of us could use them — to find campsites among stumps, to look for fish in waters heavy with silt from erosion, to search for game on ridges pounded to dust by sheep."

William O. Douglas[6]

Times have not been easy for the nation's forests since World War II. They have been the subject of bitter battles between those who would "harvest" the forests, seeing timbering and the health of the local and national timber industries as the primary purpose of the nation's forests, measuring growth and productivity only in rapid growth rather than the slower growth in older forests that others argue is the value and original purpose of having set aside national forests.

Since the Forest Service's inception, there had been no specific charter outlining the actual directive or ultimate objective of forest management. Although members of the Forest Service will claim that the multiple use philosophy directed by Pinchot had been the legal purpose attained by consensus, it was not until after World War II that that doctrine was spelled out in law from Congress.

After World War II, a new use of the forests became important to the public: recreation. The perception that the forests were being protected from timbermen who wanted to cut down the forests was dispelled as people went to the forests and found clearcutting.[7] The end of World War II marked the end — and the beginning — of another era in forestry: with the forests' size set, boundaries delineated and limits known, and with the west no longer a frontier society with few people and vast resources, demands made on the forests and management became a question of allocation of limited reserves among many uses, rather than acquisition and appropriation of ever-increasing reserves to the few interested in them. That the United States had decided to indeed retain a national forest system rather than eventually dispose of the reserves to private industry was further affirmed by the Multiple Use Act of 1960 and by NEPA, the National Environmental Policy Act, of 1970: two legislative overhauls which provided the Forest Service with guidelines and standards for using the nation's forests.

Of the post-World War II era, there are three (at the least) policy markers we can look at that have affected today's debate over use of the national forests. The first is the Sustained Yield Act of 1944. The notion of sustained yield in forest management was originally defined biologically: for every tree cut another could be planted to replace the loss and thus the country would never run out of timber. In 1944, the focus of sustained yield was shifted from timber to the timber industry: a continuous production of lumber for industry rather than just a continual renewal of trees to maintain the forests. The result was the Sustained-Yield Forest Management Act which enabled the Forest Service to enter into long-term agreements with lumber companies, and promised a constant supply of public timber to feed company mills. The guarantee was promised only when local "community stability required federal timber not available through conventional sales."[8]

Then, in 1960, the Multiple Use-Sustained Yield Act was passed through Congress. It was the first specifically stated measure to delineate just what interests should be taken into account when managing the nation's forests. The Multiple Use Act stated that the "national forests are established and shall be administered for outdoor recreation, range timber, watershed, and wildlife and fish purposes." As historian Harold Steen notes, "the law defined multiple use as utilization of resources in combination to meet needs and stipulated that economic return was not in all cases to be the limiting factor."

The issues of clearcutting in the nation's forests and of building a network of timber roads through previously unroaded forests came to the forefront as people realized that they had erroneously equated the preservation inherent in the National Park System with the purpose of the National Forests System. The last major act that had effect on recent and future management of the forests was NEPA, the National Environmental Policy Act of 1970. It required environmental impact statements to be assessed for federal legislation or agency programs affecting the forests.

Perhaps the most dynamic change toward the nation's forests was in the peoples' perception of the reserves, which contributed to the passage of the Wilderness Act in 1964. Over the sixty years in which the Forest Service has managed the forests in the west, the land has moved from a wilderness, largely inaccessible and seemingly infinite in potential material, to an island of resources — commodities of lumber and timber now meant to sustain an industry. With the increase in recreational use in the post-war era, the forests seemed fragile. They no longer were a threat to development of the western lands nor a place that posed danger to man. The forests were seen more as something to protect, valuable simply for the enjoyment found in a day's hike through a pine forest. The limits of the previously unmapped, vast forests of the west are now known. Although the forests are open to a multiplicity of uses, the desire remains among the majority of Americans to use them for what they are in their most basic form: a forest. The question facing us now is how to decide the balance between these uses.

USES OF THE FORESTS

In 1984, Congress funded the Forest Service to prepare to sell some 11 billion board feet. The Forest Service offered 11.3 billion and actually sold 11.1 billion board feet for 774 million dollars. Eighty percent of that timber came from the forests of the western U.S. Again, those are big numbers. Broken down, a board foot is the equivalent of one square foot of wood, one inch thick. In the average pine tree in the Rocky Mountains — a

Lodgepole Pine, for example — some seventy to eighty board feet are produced from the average tree 70 feet tall and 12 inches in diameter. The pines of the Pacific Northwest are much taller and thicker due to the better growing conditions found there as compared with the harsh climate of the high Rockies. The sale in 1984 would be a rough equivalent to some 158 million trees cut. The Forest Service spent 1.4 billion dollars on the sales in operating costs, not including capital outlays and expenses.

Nationally, the forests provide twenty percent of the total timber harvested in the United States. Another 30 percent comes from lands owned by the forest industry and another 50 percent comes from other private lands. The United States imports as much timber product as we export. We import lumber and wood pulp from Canada and veneer and plywood from southeast Asia. We export, primarily to Japan from Alaska, pulp chips, paper and board products.

There has been a lot of talk in 1984-1985 about "deficit" or "below cost" timber sales — that the Forest Service is actually selling the timber for less than market value. The Forest Service is one of the first to admit that some areas are simply easier to cut and sell at a higher market value than others. The year's sale requirement is set by the Chief of the Forest Service in Washington in accordance with the National Forest Management Act plans, which in turn are based on the "projected need" of the United States under the guidance of the Sustained Yield Act, to support local mills. Because of this system of management, even timber in less-than-profitable areas still must be cut — even if it is cut at a loss to the taxpayer — in order to meet the sale quotas.

In the west, according to the Forest Service annual report, 40 percent or more of the timber was sold for less than it cost to conduct the sale in five of the seven western regions. The notable losses on the timber sales occurred in those areas where the wood was either hard to get, as in Alaska, or was of poor quality and was only able to be used for pulpwood, as in most of the Rocky Mountain and Intermountain region. In these states and regions — the states of Alaska, Colorado, Wyoming, Idaho,

Utah, and Nevada and three plains states — over 75 percent of
the wood sold was sold as a loss: it was sold for less than it cost
to put the wood up for sale. Only about half of the wood sold in
the northern regions of Idaho, Montana and North Dakota was
sold above the costs of the sales, i.e. at a profit. In the Pacific
Northwest and in California, the sale price more than covered the
sale costs.

Remember that the areas sold at a loss are the same areas
that early lawmakers warned should be put into forest preserves
for the purpose of watersheds and not necessarily for timbering.
Almost one hundred years later, these same areas are being tim-
bered, with the taxpayer — you and I — subsidizing the timber
companies to cut our wood.[9]

Roads The costs of building roads into the nation's forests so
that the timber companies can cut the wood is not included in the
sale price. That is to say, the Forest Service gives the timber
companies that buy the nation's timber a cost break in order to
make these stands of timber appealing and/or marketable.
Through the Purchaser Credit Program, the timber buyer receives timber in exchange for bulldozing and building the roads
that lead to their purchased timber stand. In 1983, timber companies put in 4,500 miles of roads in the western 13 states and
received some 73 million dollars worth of timber for their effort.
They spent a little over 16 thousand dollars per mile of road. The
Forest Service put in an additional 254 miles of roads in the forests of the western 13 states, at a cost of 11.5 million dollars —
or 45 thousand dollars per mile. On top of that, the Forest
Service also built its own roads for future sales — some 1,371
miles worth in the forests in the western 13 states.

It is a point of debate as to whom is really paying for the
building of all of these roads: just under half of the total mileage
of those roads were built in the states where the nation's forests
was sold at a direct loss. In fairness, the Forest Service says that
the roads will later benefit you and I by providing easier access
to forest regions for recreation, hunting, fire fighting and overall
management. The roads, the Forest Service says, provide easier

access to the forests. Opponents of Forest Service road building practices are quick to note that the roads prevent the area in which they are built from being considered for wilderness study or future wilderness designation. Critics add that the roads adversely impact wildlife habitat since they do offer easier access.

Then there is the question of economic waste, since it is argued that the costs of the roads are not being figured into the sales costs. What "greatest good for the greatest number" is being achieved by the taxpayer who is actually paying a timber company to cut down a tree that will take eighty to a hundred years to replace, just so the taxpayer can then pay again on the open market for the wood? Other critics of the less-than-profitable use of the nation's forests argue that the waste is inherent in the system of forestry management. "The so-called sustained yield-even-flow theory that underlies public forest management guidelines is an anachronism," notes Barney Dowdle, of the University of Washington's Department of Forestry, "and it is wasteful of both public timber wealth and taxpayers' dollars. In addition, environmental impacts are unnecessarily high — not a surprising result given that public forest resources are managed without proper regard for costs."[10]

The fundamental problem of the federal government being in the land and resource management business, argues economist William F. Hyde, is that "authority and responsibility are separated. In general, public sector activity suffers from what Hardin has labeled, in a nongovernmental setting, the tragedy of the commons. Everyone's property is no one's property. The public purse and public authority, like common pastures, are over-utilized for the benefit of the few at the cost of the many. Efficient management is elusive and hard to recognize when users do not pay and it is seldom attained."[11]

The movement of the timber sales, determined by the Federal government under the sustained yield theory of use, adversely affects the private market for timber, and insures lower prices than the nation's timber should be sold for, these economists argue. The federal management also cannot take into consideration the differences in the rate of growth and the topography of the

forests beween prime timber-growth areas like the Pacific coast
and the adverse conditions of the Rocky Mountains. Federal policy sees the west as one large block, with the major differences
lying in habitat and wilderness management requirements rather
than rate of tree growth.Timbering, however, is not the only use
of the national forests, although it can be argued that of all the
uses set forth in the Multiple Use Act, the cutting of trees has
some of the most visible impact. A short survey of some of the
other uses of the nation's forests follows.

Grazing   The Bureau of Land Management is not the only a-
gency that manages domestic stock grazing. Fourteen thousand
people holding permits grazed cattle, horses, sheep and goats on
range land within the total national forest system in 1984. Grazing is measured in something called AUMs — animal unit
months. One AUM is the amount of grazing required by a 1000-
pound cow for one month. In the western 11 states (there is no
grazing on the Forest Service lands in Alaska and there is none in
Hawaii), 7.3 million AUMs were grazed from the range, with
cattle being the primary user. Eighty-three percent of the grazing
on the Forest Service lands takes place within the western states.
     Permittees pay to use the public's range, whether on the For-
est Service lands or on BLM lands. The formula used to figure
out the price AUM in the Forest Service is tied to the costs of
production and sales of the stock, although there may be a
change in the formula by Congress during 1986. Total receipts
for grazing on Forest Service lands were 10.2 million dollars.
Again, about 83 percent of that figure is generated from the western states. As a result of the currently depressed cattle market,
Forest Service receipts from grazing have fallen over the last two
years, although grazing has not decreased. The base fee is $1.23
per month, and with market price, it was about $1.16 in 1983.
     Grazing has long been a controversial topic for both the For-
est Service and the Bureau of Land Management, but the BLM
has been more obviously in the middle of the debate. The hot
tempers of the grazing debate have focused on two issues: the
price of the AUM to graze stock (some have thought it to be

too low) and the argument that it is a right, rather than a privilege, to graze stock on the public lands.

In the early years, homesteaders and nomadic sheepherders used the nation's forests long before they were designated as national forest reserves. Grazing had spread throughout the west by 1890, the same year that the United States census noted that it was, for the first time, impossible to differentiate between the settled areas and the frontier. With the Organic Act of 1897, the government claimed it also had the right to regulate the use of the range, although remember that the act itself just gave the president authority to set up the forest reserves and never indicated what was to be done with the reserves.

Pinchot issued some 8,000 permits to use the range the first year following transfer of the forest reserves to Agriculture, but it would take a Supreme Court decision years later to affirm the government's legitimacy in regulating use of the national forest ranges and its right to charge citizens for that use. In one case, Fred Light, a Colorado rancher, challenged the Forest Service's right to regulate by turning 500 head of cattle loose to graze on the Holy Cross Forest Reserve in Colorado. He appealed to the U.S. Supreme Court, ignoring an injunction against open trespass handed to him by the U.S. District Court.[12] He lost his case in 1911.

With permitting becoming the law of the land, ranchers pushed for ten-year permits in the 1920s to provide more economic stability. Part of the requirement for holding a permit served to protect their interests: you had to show your ability to sustain your stock on other lands besides Forest Service land. This requirement of "commensurability" prevented the nomadic stockmen from continuing to run herds, that were larger than the carrying capacity of the range, through the public forest range, and helped to decrease the overgrazing the Forest Service inherited when it took over the reserves.

Another result of permitting is still argued in ranching areas: that holding a grazing permit confers a property right to the permittee. The stockmen say yes. The Forest Service and BLM argue no, that it is a privilege to be able to graze on the public

ranges. We will see this issue rise again when we look at BLM
lands that are surrounded by private lands, where the land owner
basically controls access to that portion of public land.

Since 1950, the amount of grazing in the national forests
has been stable. Just as a hundred years ago, many ranchers are
still dependent upon the national forest grazing lands for their
summer range. As a side note, grazing by big game — elk, deer
and the like — is estimated to be about two-thirds the amount of
domestic stock grazing, but is not included in the AUM measurement of range carrying capacity.

Minerals/Oil/Gas The Forest Service leases 34.2 million acres
that are in the national forests for energy and mineral production
and/or exploration. In the five years from 1979 to 1983, the number of acres under lease increased by 9.5 million acres nationally.
Thirteen million barrels of oil, 205 billion cubic feet of natural
gas and 14.3 million tons of coal were produced in five years.
More than 30,000 mineral leases were processed in 1983, which
exceeds the planning goal by 43 percent. The BLM is responsible for management of the sub-surface mineral resources in
national forests, while the Forest Service is responsible for management of the surface resources, such as the timber, grazing and
wildlife. This would change if a land exchange takes place between the Forest Service and BLM.

The most hotly contested issue regarding mineral and energy development within the national forests has to do with development of leases in wilderness, habitats and land under
consideration for wilderness designation. The Forest Service
notes that there were 900 mineral or energy lease applications in
congressionally-designated wilderness areas in 1983, along with
300 applications in wilderness study areas, 700 in roadless review (RARE II) recommended wilderness study areas and
another 500 applications in RARE II further planning areas.
None of these applications were processed in 1983.

Recreation Although we may tend to think of the National Park
System when we think of recreation, a little under half of the out-

It has never been man's gift to make wildernesses. But he can make deserts, and has.

Wallace Stegner
"Wildlands in our Civilization"
1964

door recreating we do as a society takes place in the national forests. According to the annual report, 78 percent of the 228 million recreation visitor days occurred in the national forests.

It could be argued that the country first started thinking a-
bout using the vast, wild forested land of the west for recreation
rather than a frontier to be conquered when Congress ceded
lands in Yosemite Valley to California to be held "inviolate for
public use, resort and recreation," or again, in 1872, when
Yellowstone was carved out of the forests and designed as a
national park. The growing interest — or change of attitude —
toward the wild land of the west culminated in 1916 with creation of the National Park Service. The Forest Service was
already involved in recreation and resented the creation of the
Park Service because the lands that were being set aside specifically for recreation were taken from Forest Service lands, as we
will see in the section on the National Park Service. To Gifford
Pinchot, chief forester of the era, another agency for the parks
was unnecessary, and was "no more needed than two tails to a
cat."[13] The increased use of the automobile by Americans fueled
the interest in recreation on the public's lands. But the automobile offered a totally new kind of recreation experience in the
wilds of the nation's forests and national parks. As Joseph Sax
writes in his book, *Mountains Without Handrails:*

*"The kind of encounter that routinely takes place in the modern
motorized vehicle, or in the managed, prepackaged resort, is
calculated to diminish such intensity of experience. Nothing dist-
inctive about us as individuals is crucial. The margin of error
permitted is great enough to neutralize the importance of what we
know. If we roar off in the wrong direction, we can easily roar
back again, for none of our energy is expended. It isn't important to pay close attention to the weather, we are insulated from it.
We need not notice a small spring, we are not at the margin
where water counts. The opportunity for intensity of experience
is drained away. It is not that the motorized tourist or the visitor
at a highly developed site must necessarily lose intensity, or that
he is compelled to experience his surroundings at a removed*

*pace, just as it is not inevitable that backpacking or flyfishing
will produce profound, individual responses. It is rather that the
circumstances we impose on ourselves have the power to shape
our experience."[22]*

Funds to help the Forest Service deal with the people coming to visit and play in the forests did not come from Congress
until 1923, and all 10,000 dollars of it was earmarked for sani-
tation. The days of "roughing it" and the unforgettable pit toilets
of the national forests had begun. President Calvin Coolidge pub-
licized the need for a definite national policy on outdoor recreation in 1924, which resulted in the American Forestry Association and the National Park Association putting together a report
on recreation on the public's lands. It was in the joint report that
the distinction between the Forest Service and the National Park
Service was driven home: national forests represented *conservation* and national parks represented *preservation*. The report
criticized both agencies for not keeping more of their lands in a
wild condition.[15]

The boom in recreation began in earnest after World War II.
With the Multiple Use Act in 1960 mandating that recreation be
included among the recognized and designated uses of the public's forests, the stage was set for today's 157 million visitor
days. (A Recreation Visitor Day, or RVD, is the recreational use
of national forest land or water over 12 visitor hours. It could be
one person 12 hours or 12 people visiting for one hour.) The
Land and Water Conservation Fund Act of 1965 also gave the
Forest Service authority for the first time to purchase lands specifically for outdoor recreation.

Although interest in visiting the forest lands has increased,
interest in paying for it has been less enthusiastic. In 1982, the
average fee for a campsite in the National Forest System was
$3.45. In 1983 the average fee increased to $3.95. The fees for
use of national forests however, do not cover the cost of maintenance. The argument over recreational use fees resembles the
arguments stockmen originally had about their "right" to use the
public's forests versus the Forest Service's contention that it is a

privilege to use the forests, and that the cost incurred to provide
that privilege must be covered by the user. Some fees were
charged beginning in 1952, but uniform fees for specific services
were not instigated until 1965, when admission fees and user
fees could be charged. In 1972, Congress amended the collection
of fees to apply only to the National Park System and national
recreation areas. Then, in 1973, Congress amended the act again
to specifically limit user fees to the most highly developed campgrounds — those places within the forest system that had show-
ers and designated camp or trailer sites, about two-fifths of all
national campgrounds. Most recently, the user fees were increased, much to the disgruntlement of the public at large.

A discussion on recreation would not be complete without
noting the increase in the use of wilderness areas, although a ful-
ler discussion of wilderness will follow in the section on the
national parks and refuges. There is concern that with designation of some easily accessible areas as wilderness comes the
phenomena of loving the wilderness to death. Overuse of a wild
area quickly shows in rutted trails and toilet paper flags littering
the ground, and the area appears more as a playground for humans than as a pristine land truly untrammeled by humans. Even
those special interest groups who argue for more wilderness
designation note that use of the areas seems to increase with the
act of designation; it is a frustrating pattern, at best. Increased
use in some fragile areas by those who want to be in the wilderness because it is "wilderness" and not just another backpacking
experience causes the very reasons for the land to be designated
as wild land to disappear. The pattern is especially true in fragile
high alpine areas — the majority of the designated wilderness in
the forest system so far — and may occur in the fragile desert
areas as well as the BLM begins to identify and designate
wilderness in the coming years.

THE ISSUES OF THE FUTURE

The issues facing the Forest Service in the coming years are,
in one way, similar to those facing the other public lands: the

question is how to balance multiple use with ever increasing demands on national forests that are essentially static in terms of their size. The intensity of the demands on the national forests will be different from the other agencies' issues, however, because of the intensity of use the public gives the forests, both in terms of recreation and in our reliance upon the forests for natural resources. Unlike the national parks, the mission set out for the national forests is still not specifically set out; the forests are looked upon to meet all the uses and needs of society, even when many of the uses prescribed are not symbiotic.

At the base of the concerns facing the management of our national forests into the 21st century is the simple fact that we have looked at the forests as the symbol of plenty and of wealth in natural resources. They have fed our spirit as much as they have sustained our nation materially. What we, as the public, expect from the forest lands will in a great way determine whether they will become acres of cultivated timber crop or a remnant of a wild place that also provides habitat for wildlife as well as for our spirits. How will we reconcile a wooded area cut by a road system to provide needed timber, with our need for solitude? How will our children reconcile our priorities? How do we use the forests for oil and gas and coal resources? How do we reconcile the sound of seismic exploration a few miles away which carries into an area designated as "wilderness" — where we expect to be free of man's invasions of the primeval peace of a forest? How will we balance the need for timber and wood products in this country while at the same time accepting that we are not receiving market value for the product? There are no easy answers, but a solution lies in our discerning a balance of our needs and uses for the forests and our creating a land ethic of use. As Theodore Roosevelt wrote of this precarious balance:

"Conservation means development as much as it does protection. I recognize the right and duty of this generation to develop and use the natural resources of this land; but I do not recognize the right to waste them, or to rob, by wasteful use, the generations that come after us. I ask nothing of the nation except that it behave as each farmer here behaves with reference to his own

*children. That farmer is a poor creature who skins the land and
leaves it worthless to his children. The farmer is a good farmer
who, having enabled the land to support himself and to provide
for the education of his children, leaves it to them a little better
than he found it himself. I believe the same thing of a nation."* [16]

Some specific issues facing the nation's forests take us back
to the reasons for the creation of the Forest Service 100 years
ago: watershed protection and a view of the forest resources as
being for "those yet unborn" rather than a commodity to be cut at
less than market value and squandered for the immediate future.
History has not changed the fact that the west is an arid region
and watershed protection is no less important now than it was
when the preservation of forests was thought necessary for watersheds in the 1890s. It may be more important now, if only because of the increased numbers of people who live in the arid
west and thus have increased the demands upon the land for sus-
tinence. A problem that affects the original purpose of the national forests sits on the horizon: enough water for everyone in the
west. Rocky Mountain states like Colorado, Wyoming, Montana
and Utah provide the watershed and thus the water downstream
to even more arid states like Arizona, Nevada and California.

Forest policy that takes place in Colorado or Utah affects
the downstream users. One major issue facing the West on the nation's public forests is the supply of this water throughout the
West. Because of major water-works and storage projects like
the Central Arizona Project, more water will have to come from
the watersheds of the Rockies in the coming years to meet the
allocated needs in downstream states.

The Central Arizona Project, for example, was a water project that was developed on the basis of maximum flow years —
those years when runoff was highest from the Rockies. Regardless of nature's cycles and shortfalls of moisture in the Rockies
year by year, the same amount of water must still be delivered —
every year — downstream to Arizona from the up-stream watershed states. The Forest Service planned an experiment for the
summer of 1985 to see if this need can't be met continually; it
tested clear cuts within national forests to increase water runoff

for downstream users. That would mean a clear-cut area in the nation's forests in areas where clear cuts can biologically be least afforded, so that water needs for municipal and agricultural needs, as well as for backyard swimming pools, can be met in the desert.

This is not a state or a regional issue; it is the issue of highest priority use of the nation's forests. Each of us must define for ourselves the value of this kind of use: would our visit to the forests be less enjoyable or meaningful if upon our arrival, we were confronted with not a forest, but a clear cut for water users elsewhere? The early lawmakers saw the potential problem of water and opted for watershed protection; we will witness the impact of these increased watershed needs and the results of our management decisions and priorities of use of the forests by the turn of the century, according to expert estimates and predictions. It is imperative that we each consider how we want our forests used now, so that the resources are there at the turn of the century for all of our needs. Should we be demanding full market value for the resources of the forest? Or should the forests continue to be cut and sold at less than optimal value in order 1) to keep local economies afloat or 2) to provide long-term stability for timber companies while depressing the price for timber at the same time? I think the answer, again, lies in each of our individual senses of what the primary purpose of the national forests should be and how we, as people, choose to balance the multiple uses and multiple demands we place upon our forests, our sources of natural resources wealth.

Use of the forest, as with other natural resources, is a question of balance of uses. Creation of that balance is reliant upon our voicing our preferences to our local forest rangers and forest planning teams, and Congress, so that we might participate in the planning of the future of our national forests.

ROCKY MOUNTAIN NATIONAL PARK, COLORADO

II. THE NATIONAL PARKS, WILDERNESS AND WILDLIFE REFUGES
The Department of Interior

The National Park System, perhaps like no other collection of public lands, is the keystone of the public land preservation system. Within the park system are the lands that we see as being "unique," "rare," "natural wonders," and "national treasures," all worthy of special consideration and preservation. Although the quality of preservation is different, wilderness is included in this section because the thought leading to the setting aside of 24 million acres of wilderness in the west followed the same process as the thought leading to the creation of the national parks over 100 years ago. Perhaps these national parks and wilderness are the lands we picture when we think of the public lands that we, as U.S. citizens, enjoy, and which are our pride. I suspect that each of us can see in our mind's eye the views of Yosemite or Yellowstone, the Grand Canyon or Denali. Many of us have made the treks to see the national parks of the west with our families much as other cultures go at least once in their lives to a religious temple or holy place. We like to think that we have preserved the best of the United States continent in the national parks, wildlife refuges and wilderness areas — the parts that made this continent the land of wealth and opportunity that became the United States. Let's take a closer look at what we've really deposited into the national treasury and why.

NATIONAL PARKS

There are 48 parks in the National Park System; 23 of these are in the western 11 states. In Alaska, there are eight national

parks, six of which are also preserves, and four wildlife preserves. There are five national parks in Hawaii. There are also
scores of national monuments, historical sites, recreation areas,
preserves and wild and scenic rivers within the National Park
System. Nationally, all of these lands add up to some 79 million
acres within the system; 54.4 million acres of which are in Alaska. Of the 24.6 million acres left, some 20 million of them — 81
percent — are in the western states. Although the acreage seems
large, the park land set aside in the west is only six percent of the
total land mass of the west. Then there is the wilderness: 24 million acres of western land has been designated on Forest Service
land with about 342 thousand acres designated wilderness a-
mong the BLM lands so far. Wilderness designation is an on-
going process, with the BLM lands next up on the agenda for
consideration.

The park system took root with the talk about setting
Yosemite aside in 1864. Later, in 1890, when it was designated
a national park, Theodore Roosevelt noted about his experienced
during a night out in the new park:

*"Lying out at night under those giant Sequoias was like lying in a
temple built by no hand of man, a temple grander than any human
architect could by any possibility build, and I hope for the preservation
of the groves of giant trees simply because it would be a shame to civilization to let them disappear. They are monuments in themselves. In
California I am impressed by how great your state is, but I am even
more impressed by this immensely greater greatness that lies in the
future, and I ask that your marvelous natural reservations be handed on
unimpared to your posterity. It is to last through the ages."* [1]

The idea of preservation actually began in earnest with the
designation of Yellowstone as a National Park in 1872. The park
was set aside based only on the reports of few scouts and explorers who had visited the area deep in the wilds of Montana
and Wyoming territories and had talked about the "unearthly
blending of the majestic and the beautiful."

"The brain reels as we gaze into this profound and solemn
solitude. We shrink from the dizzy verge appalled, glad to feel

The national park idea represents a far-reaching cultural achievement, for here we raise our thoughts above the average, and enter a sphere in which the intangible values of the human heart and spirit take precedence. Mingled with the landscape of McKinley Park is the spirit of the primeval . . . All the plants and animals enjoy a natural and normal life without human restrictions. Freedom prevails — the foxes are free to dig burrows where they will; to hunt ptarmigan, ground squirrels and mice as the spirit moves; and they share in the ownership of the blueberry and crowberry patches. The grizzlies wander over their ancestral home unmolested; dig roots and ground squirrels, graze grass, and harvest berries to whatever menu appeals to them. The "bad" wolf seeks an honest living as of yore; he is a respected citizen, morally on a par with everyone else. His hunting of mice, ground squirrels, caribou and Dall sheep is his way of life and he has the freedom to follow it. No species of plant is favored above the rest, and they grow together, quietly competing, or living in adjusted composure. Our task is to perpetuate this freedom and purity of nature, this ebb and flow of life — first, by insuring ample park boundaries so that the region is large enough to maintain the natural relationships, and secondly, to hold man's intrusions to the minimum.

Adolph Murie
Mammals of Mt. McKinley
1962

the solid earth under our feet, and venture no more, except in forms extended and faces barely protruding over the edge of the precipice," ex-Governor Langford wrote about the Grand Canyon of the Yellowstone in 1871.

The park was set aside before any citizens could really visit it — two years before the railroad system made visiting the park anything less than a major explorer's undertaking. John Colter is believed to have been the first white man to have seen the Yellowstone area during his 500 mile solo trip through the northern Rockies during winter. Publicity that accompanied a cavalry trip made by Civil War General and former Congressman Henry Washburn, under the protection of a small Cavalry detachment led by Lt. Gustavus C. Doane, resulted in another trip being made to the area by the Geological Survey. Lt. Doane's official report said that "as a country for sightseers, it is without parallel; as a field for scientific research, it promises great results; in the branches of geology, mineralogy and ornithology, it is probably the greatest laboratory that nature furnishes on the surface of the globe."[2]

Yosemite and Sequoia were soon to follow as national parks in 1890, but not without some of the controversy and questions that still trouble the Park Service today: who or what is to be the primary beneficiary of the parks — man or nature?

A first step toward a conceptualized national park preservation system started with Teddy Roosevelt and the Antiquities Act of 1906, which enabled presidents to unilaterally set aside places of historic interest as well as "other objects of historic or scientific interest." The act was created in response to tourists looting the southwestern Anasazi ruins. Before the year 1906 was out, Roosevelt had set aside four national monuments, including the Grand Canyon in Arizona. Congress was not persuaded to make it a national park until 1919. Administrative authority was dispersed throughout the federal government until the National Park System was established in 1916, with responsibility for management of Yellowstone, Sequoia, Yosemite and General Grant National Parks falling to the War Department.

It wasn't until 1912 that some national park enthusiasts convinced President William Howard Taft that a unified national park system should be established that would encompass all of the parks, monuments and preserves. Gifford Pinchot opposed the formation of a separate parks bureau, arguing that the Forest Service was the logical agency to unify administration of the parks. In 1913, a letter of complaint was written to Interior Secretary Franklin Lane about the sorry condition of the trails in Yosemite and Sequoia and that trespass cattle were numerous within the parks. The letter also noted that creative lumbermen had managed to acquire some choice timber in Sequoia, having argued that the land was so soft from spring snowmelt that it qualified under the Swamp Land Act for dispersal to private properties. The letter was written by Steven T. Mather, descendant of a Mayflower puritan, former New York Sun reporter, and by 1913, a self-made millionaire and high-powered salesman for Twenty Mule Team Borax.[3] Lane's response was simple: If you don't like the way the parks are being run, come to Washington and do it yourself.

In 1915, Mather was sworn in as Assistant to the Secretary of Interior in charge of parks. From the moment of his appointment to office, the future of the new agency hinged on getting a bill through Congress to establish a parks bureau — and the appropriations to fund it. Mather traveled extensively throughout the United States to draw attention to the bill, then invited a carefully chosen group to visit Sequoia and Yosemite. That trip persuaded Congressional members to put up half the money to purchase the area known as Giant Forest, then in private holdings, for Sequoia National Park. The National Geographic Society put up the other half.

Mather then visited the Olympic Peninsula National Monument that Roosevelt had set aside, to talk to locals about enlarging the boundaries and potential park status for the area. It would take 23 more years and a battle pitting conservationists against lumbermen and the Park Service against the Forest Service before Olympic National Park was established.[4]

Despite national attention, no action was taken on the Park Service bill in 1915. Mather organized a national lobbying campaign that generated national public support for the idea of a national park system. President Woodrow Wilson signed the bill establishing the National Park Service on August 25, 1916. Timing was unfortunate for the new bureau, however. Just a few days after the U.S. declared war on Germany, Congress authorized a meager appropriation for the new bureau. Mather used rangers and park superintendents that were not a part of the civil service to keep costs down and to make the small appropriation go farther in setting up the new bureau. It was thought that rangers in Glacier National Park didn't patrol more than a half mile from their posts.[5] During the war, one group lobbied for the elk in Teton to be slaughtered to provide treats for the troops while Secretary Lane himself proposed that Yosemite be opened to sheep grazing. Cattle and sheep did manage to graze in the parks, but the short duration of the war prevented great damage.[6] Army troops were withdrawn from Yellowstone during the war (they had been there since 1886). Park historian Everhart notes that the military did a conscientious job in the parks and a few even resigned from the army to join the ranger's ranks.

During the early years of the Park Service, rangers did what they could with little funds and no internal promotion. "You expected to stay in the park your entire career," Everhart quotes one ranger from the early days of Mount Ranier as saying. "We longed for the stature and recognition such as had been accorded to the Forest Service. I might add that they were not always very nice to the young upstarts who had carved large chunks out of the national forests to make national parks. While they were quite quick to ridicule us for our ignorance and blunders, they really didn't know what to think of us."[7]

Automobiles were admitted to Mount Ranier in 1908. Within a few years, people were taking the cross-country tour. Everhart notes that in 1924, when Henry Ford turned out ten million "tin lizzies," there were only 12 miles of paved road in all of the national parks. Mather saw that the auto would allow more

Americans to enjoy the parks and was confident that "the experience would convert them into certified park boosters."[8] The idea of preservation of park integrity had not yet been recognized. There was a plan in the 1920s to even build dams and canals in Yellowstone to supply Idaho potato farmers with water, but the plan never came to pass, largely due to Mather's own lobbying efforts.

"Is there not someplace in this great nation of ours where lakes can be preserved in their natural state where we and all generations to follow us can enjoy the beauty and charm of mountain waters in the midst of primeval forests?" Mathers asked, while in the heat of battle against the dams.

From 1916 to 1941 was a period of basically uninterrupted growth for the National Park System, although the issues that dogged the creation of the park system continued to perplex lawmakers and petitioners for the parks: Were the parks for the enjoyment of people or for preservation unimpeded by man's tampering? Since the two appeared to be all but mutually exclusive, it was a question that was left unresolved. But the demands of time would make the need for the answer to the question more pressing and the answer more difficult.

With World War II, the park system drew to a standstill. The parks budget was cut, gasoline rationing and the temporary curtailment of auto production made tourist travel all but nonexistent. All essential park operations were discontinued and mines were opened in Yosemite. Timbering in the Olympic National Park forest was threatened until another source of Sitka spruce was found.

With the end of the war and the post-World War II explosion in tourist travel, the parks were overrun, while the budget for the park system remained at war-time levels.[9] The budget decreased again during the Korean war while tourism increased. The same parks that received 15 million visitors before the Korean war saw 54 million visitors in 1954. The assessment of the future of national parks was bleak, as a National Parks Conservations report indicates:

*"With the end of WWII, a booming economy, greater mobility, and
longer vacations combined to power a move to the outdoors such as
America had never experienced before. Restraints heretofore imposed by
geography, time, distance, and cost were, for the most part, swept aside
and with them the original simple principle from which the national
park ideal was born. The national park visit became a casual thing — of
little more significance to many than a visit to any other place that provides a scenic backdrop for everyone's outdoor thing. Appreciated? Of
course, in some way — one of a dozen vacation stops, one more decal
on the window, one more place for later comparison as to efficiency of
trailer hookup, quality of cafeteria, variety of souvenirs, and congestion
of highway and campground. The National Park was fast becomng a
playground, a bland experience, little different from what the visitor can
and does find at a thousand other places.*

*"The visitor has almost lost something else of enormous importance, a
crucial ingredient of the democratic ideal — the opportunity for choice.
He is in danger of losing the opportunity to choose the remarkable
experience which the national parks were established to save for him,
because it is in danger of disappearing."[10]*

Finally Mission 66, a ten year restoration program, was
started in the1960s to improve the sad condition of the parks for
the 50th anniversary of the system. It is reported that a photograph of a long line of tourists standing in front of a battered old
outhouse helped to encourage Congress to appropriate one billion dollars over ten years for the national parks budget. Although the fear was raised that "better facilities would bring more
people," which Everhart notes is an "accurate prediction of a
philosophical dilemma,"[11] there was little other choice if the
United States was to continue to have pride in a viable national
park system that it had originated.

WILDERNESS

The historical development of the wilderness areas
emanated from a similar desire as that which created the park
system: to preserve some of the rare and scenic areas of the
American west, simply for the value of their being unique and

beautiful and thus valuable without further development. But the battle to set aside wilderness faced a different set of hurdles, because of the era in which the campaign for wilderness preservation took place.

As the frontier closed, wilderness became an oddity instead of a threat. It became part of the public perception that wilderness — and the land in general — no longer dominated man but instead was about to be made captive of a growing, surging civilization in even the most unruly parts of the west.

"With a considerable sense of shock, Americans of the late 19th century realized that many of the forces which had shaped their national character were disappearing. Primary among these were the frontier and the frontier way of life. Long a hero of his culture, the pioneer acquired added luster at a time when the pace and complexity of American life seemed on the verge of overwhelming the independent individual," historian Roderick Nash writes.[12] With the loss of threat from the wilderness came a desire to preserve some part of it. Man could conquer wilderness, but did he really want to? The age old thrill of conquest turned out to be the thrill of pursuit of conquest rather than the thrill of the kill. Conquest came to represent a simultaneous killing of a part of ourselves which was nourished by the possibility that something wild remained for us to continually discover, rediscover, be challenged and humbled by in the face of raw nature.

"The connection between the ability of civilization to protect wilderness and the ability for civilization to survive is not so tenuous as we might wish," David Brower, a wilderness advocate and head of two environmental groups, wrote during the debate over wilderness preservation. "It is worth energetic scrutiny and at length."[13]

In truth, the battle to set aside the national parks was never far from the battle to set aside wilderness. Early proponents, such as John Muir and Aldo Leopold, were fighting for both. The connection between America's strength and character and the land was forged during the debates to save or preserve wilderness. Writers, taking a cue from Henry David ("In wildness is the preservation of the world") Thoreau, exhorted the necessary

For six years now he had heard the best of all talking. It was of the wilderness, the big woods, bigger and older than any recorded document: — of white man fatuous enough to believe he had bought any fragment of it, of Indian ruthless enough to pretend that any fragment of it had been his to convey; bigger than Major de Spain and the scrap he pretended to, knowing better; older than old Thomas Sutpen of whom Major de Spain had had it and who knew better; older even than old Ikkemotubbe, the Chickasaw chief, of whom old Sutpen had had it and who knew better in his turn. It was of the men, not white nor black nor red but men, hunters,with the will and hardihood to endure and the humility and skill to survive, and the dogs and the bear and deer juxtaposed and reliefed against it, ordered and compelled by and within the wilderness in the ancient and unremitting contest according to the ancient and immitigable rules which voided all regrets and brooked no quarter; — the best game of all, the best of all breathing and forever the best of all listening, the voices quiet and weighty and deliberate for retrospection and recollection and exactitude among the concrete trophies — the racked guns and the heads and skins — in the libraries of town houses or the offices of plantation houses or (and best of all) in the camps themselves where the intact and still-warm meat yet hung, the men who had slain it sitting before the burning logs on hearths when there were houses and hearths or about the smokey blazing of piled wood in front f stretched tarpaulins when there were not . . .

. . . It was as if the boy had already divined what his senses and intellect had not encompassed yet: that doomed wilderness whose edges were being constantly and punily gnawed at by men with plows and axes who feared it because it was wilderness, men myriad and nameless even to one another in the land where the old bear had earned a name, and through which ran not even a mortal beast but an anachronism indomitable and invincible out of an old dead time, a phantom, epitome and apotheosis of the old wild life which the little puny humans swarmed and hacked at in a fury of abhorrence and fear like pygmies about the ankles of a drowsing elephant; — the old bear, solitary, indomitable, and alone; widowered childless and absolved of mortality — old. Priam reft of his old wife and outlived all his sons . . .

William Faulkner
"The Bear"
1940

connection and thus preservation of our national character in preservation of the wilderness. Aldo Leopold, Robert Marshall,
Frederick Jackson Turner, and John Muir were early voices for
wilderness preservation beyond just the national park model.

An early battle for the Hetch-Hetchy Valley in California helped
to solidify a movement for wilderness, and brought the public into
the fray. Briefly, Hetch-Hetchy had been included in the 1890 act
creating Yosemite National Park as a wilderness preserve. San
Francisco, however, wanted the valley for a water reservoir site.
The 1906 earthquake and fire fed public sympathy for the city's
need for water, although Secretary of the Interior Ethan Hitchcock
refused to "violate the sanctity of a national park."[14] A royal battle
ensued, pitting John Muir against the more utilitarian views of
Gifford Pinchot, Teddy Roosevelt's Chief Forester. Roosevelt
reluctantly sided with use of the valley as a reservoir.

Muir then turned to the public at large to raise a hue and cry in
favor of the public's need for the spiritual haven to be found in a
wilderness such as Hetch-Hetchy. Arguing that the valley was part
of Yosemite and should not be run by private special interests in
San Francisco, a vocal opposition to Hetch-hetchy was raised. The
city retaliated, saying that the lake/reservoir would actually enhance
the wild vistas and provide more recreation for all. Through a long
battle in the public eye, the dam was finally affirmed in 1913. Although development had triumphed over wilderness in this round,
a tangible interest and insistence on preservation of the wilderness
had emerged into the public arena. The campaign to preserve wild
parts of the west and the country had not ended yet.

The next generation of wilderness advocates, including David
Brower, Howard Zanhiser, The Wilderness Society, and Olaus
Murie, began to press for wilderness that was not an "island in a
sea of civilization" as Nash puts it.

"A more important concern was to see that whatever wilderness bound-
aries there were should encompass enough of the remnant within. Wild-
erness should have the best protection man could devise in regulations,
law and ethics. In this remnant, nature indeed had rights, whether or not
the law yet recognized them; and the preservation of wilderness was one of
man's responsibilities to the planet he walks on so briefly and yearns to
see his kind survive upon." [15]

Echo Park, on the Green River in Utah, provided the show-down between development and wilderness preservation in the 1950s. Although included in Dinosaur National Monument, there was also a plan to dam the Green downstream to provide water to irrigate the arid desert country around the area. The dam was part of a ten dam, 10 billion dollar Colorado River Storage Project and would have resulted in flooding the deep canyons and gorges of the Echo Park area. Echo Park became the test case in an area where development in the heretofore empty western states was increasing. Dam construction was pending in Glacier National Park and Grand Canyon, while California was interested in Kings Canyon for a water project. The Secretary of the Interior, Oscar Chapman, approved the dam plan "in the interest of the greatest public good." In the arid, water-needing western states, and where development depended upon the ready supply of water, western congressmen could hardly not support developments like the dam. Yet, they could not ignore the flood of mail they received that was 80 to 1 against the dam. The rest of the Colorado River Project was passed in 1956.

As a result of the Echo Park victory, Howard Zanhiser, of the Wilderness Society, revived the call for a National Wilderness Preservation System and the campaign was picked up by Congress in 1957.

"The concept of a wilderness system marked an innovation in the history of the American preservation movement," Nash relates. "It expressed, in the first place, a determination to take the offensive. Previous friends of the wilderness had been largely concerned with defending it against various forms of development. But the post-Echo Park mood was confident, encouraging a bold, positive gesture. Second, the system meant support of wilderness in general rather than of a particular wild region. As a result, debate focused on the theoretical value of wilderness in the abstract, not on a local economic situation. Finally, a national wilderness preservation system would give an unprecedented degree of protection to wild country . . . The intention of the wilderness bill was to make any alteration of wilderness conditions within the system illegal."[16]

From 1957 to 1964, Congress held hearings and debated the creation of a national wilderness preservation system. Arguments over "locking up" large areas of land accessible to only a few prevailed in the debate. David Brower and other advocates warned that "all the wilderness we have now is all the wilderness we shall ever have in America." The discussion centered on the role wilderness played in forming the American character, and on an ethic of land "conservation," of "stewardship" and "trusteeship" over the land. Grassroot support was extensive, coming from people who had only a sense rather than a tangible picture of what they might be losing and might never have a chance to see were it not preserved. Mineral exploration was to be allowed in the preserved areas until January 1, 1984, according to the wilderness legislation, with valid claims open after that date if it was deemed to be in the national interest. The Wilderness Bill was passed through Congress in 1964, authorizing the creation of the preservation system, stating:

"A wilderness, in contrast with those areas where man and his own works dominate the landscape, is hereby recognized as an area where the earth and its community of life are untrammeled by man, where man himself is a visitor who does not remain."

The system continues to grow, although wilderness advocates will say privately that the 24 million acres currently designated from Forest Service lands is probably about all the wilderness that will be set aside due to competing interests in the lands. The wilderness system in the BLM lands is the campaign of the future, as is noted at the end of this chapter, but wilderness status of 13 percent of National Forest land, some 20 million acres, is also still unresolved. Twenty-one percent of the unresolved land is in Alaska. If all the land that is currently being negotiated, bargained and horse-traded over is added to the National Wilderness Preservation System, just under a third of the national forests in the west will be wilderness. Looked at from a slightly larger scale, that would be 26 percent of all of the national forest land in the United States, but it would be only five percent of all land — public and private —

in the western states. Taken one step further, it would be only 1.5 percent of the whole of the U.S. land mass, a land that was nothing but wilderness 300 years ago. The establishment of the National Wilderness Preservation System recognized that man alone was responsible for the loss of wilderness; it follows that man can — and must — act if he is to prevent his own actions from destroying the wilderness he values.

REFUGES

As with the other natural resources of the land, wildlife was considered the property of the king before the creation of the United States. After the country's independence, wildlife management was, for the most part, given over to the individual states. President Theodore Roosevelt, as conservationist and sportsman as well as president of the United States, however, was not content to let the wildlife disappear from the Western Frontier, as had the buffalo over the thirty years before his administration. "Even more important (than a list of other accomplishments during his administration) was the taking of steps to preserve from destruction beautiful and wonderful wild creatures whose existence was threatened by greed and wantonness," Roosevelt wrote in his autobiography.[17] He started by regulating the export of heads and trophies of big game from the Territory of Alaska in 1902 and 1908. In 1902, he appropriated the money for preservation of the buffalo in Yellowstone National Park. In 1905, Roosevelt set aside 12,000 acres for the Wichita Game Preserve, the first game preserve in the United States. He followed that action by setting aside 1.49 million acres for the Grand Canyon Game Preserve. He counted on the national monuments he set aside, like Muir Woods, California; Pinnacles, New Mexico; and Mount Olympus, Washington, to "form important refuges for game," as well as important sites for national monuments of scientific value. In 1906, Roosevelt enabled the passage of an act regulating the shooting of birds in the District of Columbia, making three-quarters of the District a refuge. In 1908, Roosevelt created the National Bison Range in Montana. Between 1903 and

1909, 51 bird reservations and four big game refuges were established throughout the United States, from Hawaii to Alaska to
Puerto Rico.

The total refuge system today is 90 million acres. There are
some 771 refuges in the western 13 states. Some 77 million acres of the refuge system are located in Alaska, but this acreage
does not include the combination national parks and preserves set
aside with the Alaska Lands Bill in 1980. In the western states,
California and Montana have the largest number of wildlife and
waterflow refuges, but Arizona and Montana have the largest
acreage devoted to the refuges.

In 1939, the U.S. Fish and Wildlife Service was set up to
manage these natural resources that," are a living, renewable
form of national wealth that is capable of being maintained and
greatly increased with proper management, but equally capable
of destruction if neglected or unwisely exploited; that such outdoor recreation throughout the Nation and provide employment,
directly or indirectly, to a substantial number of citizens . . ."[18]
as the act establishing the U.S. Fish and Wildlife Service states.
Hunting, fishing and the extraction of minerals and fuels are allowed on the wildlife refuges, "if they do not jeapordize the natural values," the legislation notes.

With the Alaska Lands Bill, a number of the national parks
set up in 1980 also provided acreage for wildlife preserves adjacent to the park boundaries. Sport hunting is permitted in these
preserves, although not in the national parks without subsistence
hunting permits. Of course, telling one boundary from another is
difficult in the wild and violations take place yearly, with moose,
caribou, bear and wolves being hunted and killed within the national parks. The park rangers do all they can in monitoring these
wild areas of Alaska and acknowledge their frustration at not always preventing such "mistakes."[19] There are also simple preserves and refuges in Alaska: a total of 16, 10 of which are also
wilderness areas.

Before we examine the issues of management and care of
the national parks and refuges and wilderness areas which we
will face in the coming years, a note should be made about the

differences among the lands. The specific expectations each of us
hold when we visit the wilderness, compared with a visit to the
national parks, is where the similarity between the two types of
public land ends. Although each of us expects to see nature, the
way in which we experience nature is markedly different. It is
estimated, for example, that only five percent of the people who
visit the national parks ever leave the roadside or developed areas
within the parks. No figure is available on how many visitors actually get farther than a quarter mile away from their car for any
length of time, but 95 percent of park visitors never see most of
the remote areas inside the national parks. (National Park Service
staff note with some amusement that the only thing that would
irk a "preservationist" more than the nominal use of the backcountry in parks by the automobile public is seeing the other 95
percent of the visitors on the trails and in the parks backcountry.)

For most of us who visit the national parks, we expect to
see nature with a sense of security, control or protection. It is, in
fact, sometimes difficult to convince the visiting public that the
land and the wildlife within the parks are wild and are not part of
a city park, zoo or museum experience. The atmosphere of the
parks only contributes to this perception by visitors passing
through in the comfort and safety of their cars and recreational
vehicles. Signs throughout Yellowstone prepare visitors for
"wildlife exhibit" turnouts and parking areas, as well as scenic
overlooks and wildlife overlooks. To see a herd of buffalo or elk
placidly grazing in a meadow just beyond a sign reading "wildlife exhibit" can placate the keenest sense of caution in reacting to
the wildlife. It is no wonder that rangers spend the majority of
their time telling visitors to come — slowly — from the middle
of grazing buffalo herds, to not stick a camera in the face of the
buffalo and reminding people that the animals are wild and thus
potentially dangerous.

The park experience at night is vastly different from the
wilderness experience as well. In the park campgrounds during
summer season, complete with running water, camper facilities
and electric plugs, the blue glow of televisions in RVs light up
the dark night as brightly as the stars or a full noon. The night is

*T*he tendency nowadays to wander in
wildernesses is delightful to see. Thousands of tired, nerve-shaken, over-
civilized people are beginning to find out that going to the mountains
is going home; that wildness is a necessity; and that mountain parks
and reservations are useful not only as fountains of timber and irrigating rivers, but as fountains of life. Awakening from the stupefying
effects of the vice of over-industry and the deadly apathy of luxury,
they are trying as best they can to mix and enrich their own little on-
goings with those of Nature, and to get rid of rust and disease. Briskly
venturing and roaming, some are washing off sins and cobweb cares of
the devil's spinning in all-day storms on mountains; sauntering in
rosiny pinewoods or in gentian meadows, brushing through chaparral,
bending down and parting sweet, flowery sprays; tracing rivers to their
sources, getting in touch with the nerves of Mother Earth; jumping
from rock to rock, feeling the life of them, learning the songs of them,
panging in whole-souled exercise and rejoicing in deep, long-drawn
breaths of pure wildness. This is fine and natural and full of promise.
And so also is the growing interest in the care and preservation of
forests and wild places in general, and in the half-wild parks and
gardens of towns. Even the scenery habit in its most artificial forms,
mixed with spectacles, silliness, and kodaks; its devotees arrayed more
gorgeously than scarlet tanagers, frightening the wild game with red
umbrellas, even this is encouraging and may well be regarded as a
hopeful sign of the times.

All the Western mountains are still rich in wildness, and by means of good roads are being brought nearer to civilization every year. To the sane and free it will hardly seem necessary to cross the continent in search of wild beauty, however easy the way, for they find it in abundance wherever they chance to be. Like Thoreau they see forests in orchards and patches of huckleberry brush, and oceans in ponds and drops of dew. Few in these hot, dim, frictiony times are quite sane or free; choked with care like clocks full of dust, laboriously doing so much good and making so much money — or so little — they are no longer good themselves.

When, like a merchant taking a list of his goods, we take stock of our wildness, we are glad to see how much of even the most destructible kind is still unspoiled. Looking at our continent as scenery when it was all wild, lying between beautiful seas, the starry sky above it, the starry rocks beneath it, to compare its sides, the East and the West, would be like comparing the sides of a rainbow. But it is no longer equally beautiful. The rainbows of today are, I suppose, as bright as those that first spanned the sky; and some of our landscapes are growing more beautiful from year to year, notwithstanding the clearing, trampling work of civilization. New plants and animals are enriching woods and gardens and many landscapes wholly new, with divine sculpture and architectures are just now coming to the light of day as the mantling folds of creative glaciers are being withdrawn, and life in a thousand cheerful, beautiful forms is pushing into them, and new-born rivers are beginning to sing and shine in them. The old rivers, too are growing longer like healthy trees, gaining new branches and lakes as the residual glaciers at their highest sources on the mountains recede, while their rootlike branches in their flat deltas are at the same time spreading farther and wider into the seas and making new lands . . .

Man, too, is making may far-reaching changes. This most influential half animal, half angel is rapidly multiplying and spreading, covering the seas and lakes with ships, the land with huts, hotels, cathedrals, and clustered city shops and homes, so that soon, it would seem, we may have to go farther than Nansen to find a good sound solitude. None of Nature's landscapes are ugly so long as they are wild; and much, we can say comfortingly, must always be in great part wild, particularly the sea and the sky, the floods of light from the stars, and the warm, unspoilable heart of the earth, infinitely beautiful, though only dimly visible to the eye of imagination. The geysers, too spouting from the hot underworld; the steady, long-lasting glaciers on the mountains, obedient only to the sun; Yosemite domes and the tremendous grandeur of rocky canons and mountains in general — these must always be wild, for man can change them and mar them hardly more than can the butterflies that hover above them . . .

These grand reservations should draw thousands of admiring visitors at least in summer, yet they are neglected as if of no account, and spoilers are allowed to ruin them as fast as they like. A few peeled spars cut here were set up in London, Philadelphia and Chicago, where they excited wondering attention; but the countless hosts of living trees rejoicing at home on the mountains are scarce considered at all. Most travelers here are content with what they can see from car windows or the verandas of hotels, and in going from place to place cling to their precious trains and stages like wrecked sailors to rafts. When an excursion into the woods is proposed, all sorts of dangers are imagined, snakes, bears, Indians. Yet it is far safer to wander in God's woods than to travel on black highways or to stay at home. The snake danger is so slight it is hardly worth mentioning. Bears are a peaceable people, and mind their own business, instead of going about like the devil seeking whom they may devour. Poor fellows, they have been poisoned, trapped, and shot at until they have lost confidence in brother man, and it is not now easy to make their acquaintance. As to Indians, most of them are dead or civilized into useless innocence. No American Wilderness that I know of is so dangerous as a city home 'with all the modern improvements.' One should go to the woods for safety, if for nothing else.

John Muir
January 1898

filled with the sound of radios and other forms of musical enter-
tainment as campers sleep less than fifty feet from their autos.
Both rangers and visitors agree that this is the kind of experience
many people seek in the national parks — one of a safe and struc-
tured visit with the out-of-doors. Who is to say that this form of
communion with nature is any less an "experience" than that of
the backpacker in the wilderness; it is simply different.

Yet there are responsibilities that accompany each of these
experiences that have to do with the ethics of visiting the wild
lands. The influx of people to a park, like the relative overuse of
40 people using a wilderness access area, needs to be managed
to prevent serious harm or destruction to the environment — the
reason why people ventured to see the wild lands in the first
place. Nothing can ruin an outdoor experience faster than the trail
of trash or flashbulbs or toilet paper markers left by a previous
visitor to either wilderness or park. In dealing with the wild
lands, the basic problem is "how to enjoy it today and still have it
tomorrow," as Brower notes.[20]

"Engagement with nature provides an opportunity for detachment from the submissiveness, conformity, and mass behavior that dogs us in our daily lives; it offers a chance to express
distinctiveness and to explore our deepest longings. At the same
time, the setting — by exposing us to the awesomeness of the
natural world in the context of 'ethical recreation' moderates the
urge to prevail without destroying the vitality that gives rise to it:
to face what is wild in us and yet not revert to savagery," writes
Joseph L. Sax in his book on the national park experience,
Mountains Without Handrails.[21]

One of the conundrums of the park or wilderness experience is the need for regulation to prevent man from destroying
that which he sought to experience; yet the idea of regulation of
one's actions in the wild is at best a dichotomy. It is like the questions surrounding the building of a bridge over a river in a wilderness area. Its purpose is to prevent further destruction of a fragile area, yet with its very existence, a piece of the wilderness is
in fact impinged upon by man and nature, and is not left alone.

The conflict between man and use of nature is best seen in

the parks. It is the old question of whether the parks are primarily for the enjoyment of people or for the preservation of the wild, when the two objectives are in conflict at some level of interaction. It is tempting to beg the questions this conflict raises, and allow the national parks to continue on as they have for 70 years, balancing through each day by responding to immediate needs and problems without defining clear solutions to the conflict in philosophy. In reality, the conflict is magnifying in some of the western national parks where, in order to preserve areas of the wilderness, some choices about priorities and designated use must be made. The prime example is Yellowstone, where certain areas and trails are closed off to human use during certain times of the season so that the grizzly bear may use the areas without man's intervention or distraction. Another use plan in Yellowstone National Park takes the issue a step further: the Park Service published plans to close a camping and shopping facility within the park known as Fishing Bridge. The goal of the planned closure was to let the area revert back to the prime grizzly habitat once was. It is critical habitat for the grizzly bear in spring and summer. The decision was not happily welcomed by human users of the area who liked the development. The imminent closure immediately raised the question of whether the parks were for people or bears and wildlife habitat in general. Although the plans remain intact to close Fishing Bridge, the final solution has yet to be seen — as the battle for use continues.

Other concerns surround the fear that wilderness and some national parks have become isolated oases, habitats for wildlife, as development outside the parks — not just mineral and energy, but urban as well — surrounds the borders of the preserved areas. There is still the feeling in areas of the west that wildlife and predators such as grizzly, black bear, wolf and cougar find sanctuary in the forests and national parks, don't belong outside those park boundaries. The rangers and wildlife managers that deal with habitat questions are fond of saying that "Bears (or other predators of which man has been traditionally afraid) and people don't mix and it is the animal that always loses." It is odd that since man has become comfortable with the fact that the wilderness is no longer a specific danger to our existence, the wildlife that were equally feared as part of the wilderness have not yet been accepted as an indigenous part of the wilderness. We have yet to recognize that an encounter between man and bear is equally life-threatening and that cautious avoidance is the best management philosophy for survival of both endangered or threatened predators such as bear and wolf as well as man.

Let's take as an example the Yellowstone ecosystem. Yellowstone Park itself is 2.2 million acres — larger than Delaware and Rhode Island combined. The adjacent Grand Teton National Park adds another 300,000 acres of forest and peaks to the park area. Around those two parks is 6 million acres of land partially managed by the Forest Service, as well as by the states of Montana, Wyoming and Idaho. The area in its entirety, without the imposition of the imaginary park, national forest and state boundaries, represents an ecosystem or a biological unit — an entire habitat for certain plant and animal species.

A movement has begun to encourage designation of the entire area as an ecosystem and to unify management of the area under one agency with one objective: wildlife habitat. Around the park boundaries within the national forests are some 50 oil and gas exploratory wells, mineral mines, geothermal projects and timbering areas. Members of the Greater Yellowstone Ecosystem Coalition, the group that is advocating the unified management plan, argue that these developments constitute a threat to the integrity of the entire habitat.

Wildlife do not recognize the artificial boundaries man has delineated and make use of all of the forested areas they can. Their movement is limited by their biological range — the area they depend upon to provide food and habitat for their survival — and by man's presence in the area. Under current management by the various agencies and states, bears and other predators that are perceived as a threat to man or livestock can be removed. The wildlife agencies are trying to move bear, for example, away from where they are causing a disturbance. The grizzly bear is protected and cannot be willfully destroyed, but if bears continue to present a problem to locals, the usual fate for the animal is to be destroyed.

The coalition movement is young, but recognition by Congress, as a biological unit under one management plan with the goal of habitat, would be a first for land-use policy in the coninental United States. It would be the first time in history that all of the land-use agencies and departments, state and federal, would unify under one management plan.

Another side of the habitat question is the reintroduction of species that have already been eradicated from these wild habitats. The Forest Service and the National Park Service, for example, are currently looking at reintroducing the grey wolf to Glacier National Park in Montana and possibly in Yellowstone and Rocky Mountain National Park as well. The wolf used to range over those areas as natural habitat, but was eradicated by man both in and out of the parks. Rocky Mountain National Park leadership, at the moment, has taken the philosophy that it will protect the species if it naturally recurs, but is not eagerly looking to reintroduce the wolf. "Why impose that kind of pain on the wolf" Rocky Mountain Park Superintendent James Thompson asks. The wolf has a large ranging area and would face extermination again by humans if it left park boundaries. Man's stigma or fear regarding the wolf still runs rampant, it seems. Man's perception of the wolf does not consider the dominant position man maintains in the west these days.

Another issue facing the parks and wilderness areas in the coming years is how much we are willing to pay for the experience of using the parks or wilderness areas. Access to the wilderness is basically free and only a small charge ($2 for a week) is necessary to enter the parks; yet many of us have spent entire vacations behind a $22,000 recreational vehicle on the park roads while backpackers and campers willingly spend thousands of dollars on backcountry equipment. Two questions arise regarding the value of the use of the lands by recreational users: Are we willing to pay more to have use of these lands? Are we willing to pay increased fees that would go into wildlife management or park improvements? Secondly, are we willing to set a limit on the number of visitors allowed in an area in a given season — a sort of self-regulating measure — to help to preserve the area and lessen the irreparable damage that accompanies heavy human use of the fragile tundra and wilderness lands. A limit on the number of camping permits available during the busy summer season is already in effect in many of the wilderness areas in the west and in the national parks. To be more effective, more self-regulating may be necessary for wilderness areas that are easily accessible by auto and foot.

Man's presence is the factor that has caused the areas of wilderness to shrink, and has necessitated the camping permit process in parks and designated wilderness areas. Equally, it is man's self-management in response to the value of preserving some of these lands that has enabled a piece of the wilderness to remain for us to enjoy today and for the future.

"That basic choice remains with us — whether we circle back to the original concept or permit further spin off into stultifying medioc-rity.The choice is ours, whether the parks shall remain "crown jewels" of our outdoor heritage to be cherished, protected, preserved and worthy of our rigorous self-imposed restraints, or be permitted to denegrate into the common place. It is a difficult choice, but it must be made. And nobody else can make it. The choice is ours alone."[22]

That was the assessment of the *Report on National Parks for the Future* in 1972. The questions facing us over the next 25 years remain the same and are more pressing, as use of the parks and wilderness areas increase while the possibility of set-ting aside larger parcels of wildland all but escapes the realm of our choices. Because of widespread development, roads and timbering in the national forests, little other land meets the stan-dards of wilderness or national park. BLM desert and grass lands are among the last choices we have to set the land aside in our wilderness preservation system.

Wilderness is not forever; it is always available for later use if we deem it necessary, but those are choices made available to us only by our judicious setting aside of lands into wilderness now. Further preservation of the wilderness, whether in parks or wilderness areas, is totally within our control. The choice of banking our lands is a luxury we cannot afford to squander through indecision or apathy.

RED DESERT, BLM LAND, WYOMING

III. THE BUREAU OF LAND MANAGEMENT
The Department of Interior

The lands of the Bureau of Land Management are known as the "lands nobody wanted," because they were the lands left over after homesteading and claimstaking had taken place. They were literally the lands nobody wanted to homestead, because they were too dry, too rocky, the climate too arid, too harsh, or simply the lands were too hard to do anything with. But as it has turned out over these last 50 years since they were removed from public offering, they are the lands nobody wants to own, but the lands everybody, it seems, is interested in leasing.

Stockmen lease grazing rights for their cattle, horses and sheep; oil, gas and coal companies lease the subsurface development rights. They are the lands where the deer and antelope play — or don't, as access to some of the BLM acres is restricted by private ranchers' fences or surrounded by private land which become in effect private hunting preserves, although the land itself is still publicly owned. They are also increasingly the lands where the public plays, in off-road vehicles, on dirt bikes and other recreational uses of the grass and desert areas. Some of the land — a fraction of one percent — has been set aside as wilderness. Members of the environmental lobby see the BLM lands as the next battleground for wilderness designation in the future, arguing that even the lands nobody wanted to live on have a value that makes them worth preserving as an ecosystem and as part of the heritage of this country. Maybe it is more accurate to say that the BLM lands are those lands in which no one has a passionate interest. Perhaps the sage and stubble of gramma and buffalo grass of the plains of some dry western states comes to mind when picturing the BLM lands. Certainly, some of these lands have no obvious scenic value when compared to Yellowstone or

the Bob Marshall wilderness in Montana, but to compare them is
a disservice to the unique character of the BLM lands. Rocky deserts, badlands like the Bisti Wilderness in Arizona are part of the
BLM lands as well. The BLM lands are of subtle beauty, hidden
in the quiet of a desert or the vast grassland beneath a deep blue
sky. You have to really stop and look at the lands to see their special qualities and enjoy the values they offer. Once you are past
the lack of trees, forests and high mountain streams, you can begin to see their beauty instead of only sagebrush and cactus.

The Bureau of Land Management manages 340.6 million
acres of land in the western twelve states (there is no BLM land
in Hawaii). A little less than half of that acreage is in Alaska.
Yet, consider that the 173.6 million acres located in the lower 48
states is about the same size as the total area of Montana and Wyoming put together plus the northern third of Colorado. The land
is divided between grazing districts, mineral and gas and oil
lands. Only six percent is being studied for wilderness at present, although the big push for more recommendations for wilderness is just beginning. The BLM also manages some forests —
1.7 million acres of the old Oregon and California railroad grants
in western Oregon as well as six million other acres throughout
the west.

Before oil and gas and coal became important to the United
States, grazing was the primary purpose of the BLM. Since passage of the 1920s Mineral Leasing Act, energy and minerals
revenues represented over 70 percent of BLM's total revenues.
BLM is in charge of all minerals management on the federal
lands. With the leasing of the Outer Continental Shelf, beginning
in 1950, the mineral leasing represents consistently over 90 percent of the agency's revenues. Still, it was grass — or lack of it
— that provided the energy for creation of the bureau.

According to some historians, the emergence of the Grazing
Service was the natural evolution toward the land in the mid-to-
late 1800s. With Lincoln's signing of the Homestead Act in
1860, the way was paved for any citizen, 21 years of age or a
head of household, to acquire title to 160 acres with a small title
fee and construction of improvements on the land. The problem

was that as the settlers moved into the high, arid rangeland of the west, no family could subsist on 160 acres. Crops wouldn't grow and 160 acres didn't provide enough forage for a cattle or sheep operation. The Desert Land Act of 1873 increased the claim amount of some range lands that were available for homesteading to 640 acres. It was a reflection of the government attempting to make policy to match the land homesteaders were finding as they moved west of the 100th Meridian. Under the Desert Land Act, certain parcels of 640 acres would be made available to the homesteaders if they could irrigate it within three years. Fraud abounded, with some cattle companies building canals where there was no water and where topographically, they couldn't irrigate even if there had been any water. No Washington authority ventured out west to see if the land had actually been irrigated, so much of the land remained in private hands under the claims.[1]

"The result of 'free land' had to be overgrazing," notes historian Philip Foss. "If there was any grass left (after you finished grazing it), other stockmen would take it."[2] It was a case of the "tragedy of the commons,"* run amuck.

Because the non-mountainous land in the west is best suited to grazing, the early ranchers and cattle companies maintained free rein in staking out the empty, wide open spaces for themselves. J. F. Glidden's invention of barbed wire in 1874 helped the stockmen to take control of the public domain range. Some stockmen had already moved to claim and thus "own" key tracts of the range — *i.e.* where the water was, leaving the range around it useless to any other ranchers. Some stockmen had already erected fences across the public domain in the ten years after the invention of barbed wire. Foss reports that two Colorado ranchers had fenced one million acres each, while in New Mexico, three million acres had been fenced in two counties.

---

* *The "tragedy of the commons" is an expression which refers to the tragedy of no one person taking responsibility for their personal use of land held in the common trust. Garret Hardin wrote about it in his 1968* Science *article, "The tragedy of the Commons."*

*I*t was a strange land, and all its strangeness came from the simple arithmetic of its rainfall. A grudging land — it gave reluctant crops only. A treacherous land — its thin rain might fail without reason or warning, and then there were no crops at all and the pioneer who had been ignorant of drouths, promptly starved. An inventive land — besides drought it had other unprepared-for plagues: armies of locusts and beetles, rusts and fungi never encountered in the forests, parasites that destroyed grains and cattle which had been habituated to an Eastern climate. A poisoned land — it was laboriously salted with strange earths which must be leached away before seeds could germinate. And in the end as in the beginning, a dry land — so that all problems returned to the master probem of how to get enough water on land for which there could never be water enough. In sum, conditions that made unavailing everything that the pioneers had learned, conditions that had to be mastered from scratch if the last frontier was to be subdued.

And, therefore, the final strangeness of the West: it was the place where the frontier culture broke down. The pioneer's tradition of brawn and courage, initiative, individualism, and self-help was unavailing here. He could not conquer this land until history caught up with him. He had, that is, to ally himself with the force which our sentimental critics are sure he wanted to escape from: the Industrial Revolution . . .

The pioneer might cut sod or mold adobe bricks for a shanty, but he could not fence his claim until industrialism brought him barbed wire.

The Plains Indians were better equipped than he for the cavalry campaigns that had to be the West's warfare — so the Industrial Revolution had to give him repeating rifles and repeating pistols, especially the latter. So far as the Winning of the West was a war of conquest, victory waited upon the Spencer, the Winchester, and especially the Colt. And always the first condition: to grow crops where there was not water enough. The Revolution's railroads had to bring westward the Revolution's contrivances for deep cultivation, bigger and tougher plows, new kinds of harrows and surfacers and drills, and its contrivances for large-scale operations, new harvesters and threshers, steam and then gasoline group-machines which quadrupled cultivating power and then quadrupled it again. Finally, the problem of the water itself. The axe swinging individualist had farmed his small claim with methods not much different from those of Cain's time. The Western pioneer could not farm at all until the Revolution gave him practicable windmills, artesian wells, and the machinery that made his dams possible. When he crossed the hundredth meridian, in order to be Cain at all he had first to become Tubal-Cain. Meanwhile the government, the press, the whole nation were expediting the rush of settlement. It was Zeitgeist, by God!

The continent had to be occupied — a bare spot on the map was an affront to the eagle's children. The folk migration, now in its last phase, was speeded up. Manifest destiny received the valuable assistance of high-pressure publicity.

Bernard DeVoto
1934

In 1884, President Cleveland himself had to order the re-
moval of all of the fences on the public domain land that ranchers
had built, taking *defacto* control over the land without actually
owning it. Without the fences, the ranchers lost their control to
the nomadic sheep-herders that were helping to strip the range
clean of grass. [3] The rancher, undaunted, rebuilt their fences
when the federal marshalls returned east, but the time was coming when the homesteaders would pinch the stockmen's free
rein of the west with their homesteads. Ironically, the homesteaders, too, ended up grazing as there was little else they could
do with the land. "With many competitors for disputed open
range, each individual had incentive to stock the land heavily and
harvest it rapidly before others could do so," observes economist
Gary Libecap.[4]

Homesteaders who tried dryland farming plowed the range
sod-side sown, soil side exposed to the elements (known as the
"wrong side up," out west). Their farms failed and the homesteaders had to move on, abandoning the land and leaving it
totally useless, even for grazing. Montana ranchers today still
relate with rueful tone in their voices the actions of the homesteaders and how the land is just now, 60 years later, returning
to what some refer to as "some decent grazing grass."

Yet, even by 1916 and the Stockraising Homesteaders Act,
which made 640 acres the standard claim for all range lands, the
rancher and stockmen were still seen as "a crude forerunner of
civilization of which the farmer was the advance guard and the
hoe the symbol."[5]

By 1934, 25 million acres of western range had been
plowed up and abandoned. That year, an executive order was
signed withdrawing all public land from public homesteading in
Arizona, California, Colorado, Idaho, Montana, New Mexico,
Nevada, Oregon, Utah and Wyoming. An estimated 50 million
acres of relatively good range land had become submarginal crop-
land. At the turn of the century, the stockmen had seen what was
coming and had started to lobby for leasing of all public lands
that were to be used for grazing. Some kind of management
and/or regulation was needed. Although they had previously

formed into grazing associations privately,[6] the federal intervention into their controlling access to the lands had muted the
effects their stock associations had on the public lands.

"At this time, there are large areas where it is a free-for-all
and general grab-and-hold-it-if-you-can policy with roving herds
using the range," a rancher testified in the debate of the Grazing
Act. "There is no security of safety to honest stock business. We
have had many sheep and cattle wars. For many years there has
been more or less a kind of guerrilla warfare going on between
and among the sheepmen and cattlemen with bitterness, strife, ill-
will, and more or less litigation, and some sad killings."[7]

Although the Frontier had been declared closed in 1890, it
took until 1934 to pass the Taylor Grazing Act, which would regulate the BLM range lands. With passage of the act, however, an
old battle reemerged: What the cattle companies and ranchers had
known as their right to use the public lands for grazing suddenly
became a privilege for which they had to pay. Despite the
commencement of needed management that accompanied the act,
the new law represented a change in the quality and freedom of
land use and availability in the west. Preferences for grazing
privileges were given to the land and not to the people.

By 1936, the grazing districts had been enlarged to include
142 million acres, with the new Division of Grazing (name
changed in 1939 to the Grazing Service) in charge of leasing and
management. Although the lands had a wide diversity of topography and climate, ranging from desert to sage and higher-ele-
vation plains, 95 percent of the land under the control of the new
agency received (and still does) less than 15 inches of annual
rainfall. As with the Forest Service, exactly what the federal government was now landlord over wasn't really known, except by
the ranchers who had been using the land for the fifty years before the Grazing Service had been established. "There were no
maps of the domain — believe it or not," noted Farry Carpenter,
former Colorado rancher and first chief of the Division of
Grazing.[8] "The status changed every hour as entries were made
The only people who know where the remaining public lands
were and what they were, were the stockmen who used them and

*W*hat does ownership of land mean *after all? It simply means that I have a life lease on it. I can't take it with me and I can't run it after I'm gone, so at best, ownership is just for a man's lifetime. He's just a custodian. With the gigantic changes in our social structure that are facing us today, don't think for a minute that the land is not going to be put in the hands of the people who can make use of it.*

Now what about management of this land? Walter Heller, the economist who was an adviser to President Kennedy but has now returned to the University of Minnesota, said that the federal government can govern but it can't administer. Why can't it administer? Because it can't get close enough to the people that are to be administered. That face contributed to the dissolution of the British Empire: England could govern, yes, but it could not administer — simply because the sun never set on the British Empire. And we have come around in our own way to see that after all, administration must come from the home folks.

I remember when the Taylor Grazing Act was first passed. We set out to do something with it, and knowing nothing about the area except the little spot of land where I live, I rushed over to the General Land Office and said, "I am going out there to handle 140,000,000 acres of land and I would like to know where it is. You have all the records. I'd like to have a map."

"We haven't any map."

"What? No map?" I said. "You've been administering this land a hundred years longer than the Department of the Interior has existed and you don't even have a map! What kind of outfit is this?"

Well, the fellow looked at me like a bull at a bastard calf. He said, "You don't know much, do you? We can't map the public domain. We have seventeen land offices in the West and they are open as the sun goes around. Every minute of the day, some bird is walking in and homesteading a piece — Timber and Stone entry, Cary Act land election, mining claims. So it changes every minute. We never know what it is. The fellows out there have their township plates. They send us copies every month, then we take a couple of years to look them over, and so they just go on, though nobody knows where the land is."

"How do you expect me to administer it when I don't know where it is?"

"Well," he said, "You wanted the job and it pays a good salary."

F.R. Carpenter.
First Director, Div. of Grazing
U.S. Dept. of Interior
1970

they had first hand and accurate knowledge."

The Grazing Service merged with the old General Land Office to create the Bureau of Land Management in 1946. The Dust Bowl that had sent scores of homesteaders back to the east or on to California was finally over. The 180 million acres of land that had been designated as "unreserved and unappropriated land" were closed to homesteading in 1933. Before 1930, the sales of those lands had averaged one million acres per year since 1850. Sales decreased to less than one million acres in the 1930s. The great rush to the west, the land of promise, had been over for 16 years and to those who had been staking their un-official claims on the range lands in the west for 75 years, it was the end of an era.

The Taylor Grazing Act set up a fee formula whereby ranchers would be charged for the amount of grass their stock used. A measure of animal units per month (AUM) was set (meaning the amount of forage one animal unit would eat in a month). The BLM glossary defines an animal unit as "one cow equals one horse equals five sheep equals five goats equals four reindeer, all over the age of six months." Because the free-roaming buffalo had been exterminated on the plains (the only surviving population remained in Yellowstone National Park), the amount of forage the creatures eat is not included in the animal unit. The grazing act itself set out the directives for the Grazing Service and subsequently, for the BLM:

"To stop injury to the public grazing lands by preventing overgrazing and soil deterioration, to provide for their orderly use, improvement and development, to stabilize the livestock industry dependent upon the public range, and for other purposes."[9]

The creation of the fee, based on the AUM, strengthened the stockmen's feeling that they were now paying for what had been a right and had been free. In December 1934, commenting on the creation of fees, Farry Carpenter noted:

*"If we charge no fee, it would amount to government sub-
sidy, and a government subsidy is always subject to scrutiny,
criticism and investigation. You stockmen should set some fair
fee, so that you can go before any committee from Boston or
Newport, or anywhere else, and show it is fair. Otherwise you
are never going to be away from constant criticism from the
people in the east and the middle west who feel that the way to
solve the question is to throw all the cattle and sheep off of the
public domain . . . So, we will want fees for our own protection.
The only kind of a fee which ever met with any degree of satisfaction on the part of stockmen is that such as they have in the
forests, based on a sliding scale whereby it is apportioned ac-
ording to the price of beef and mutton. In other words, the
expenses should be in accord with the income."[10]*

Although the Grazing Service maintained a flat fee of five
cents per cow or horse grazed (one cent per sheep) until 1943,
both of Carpenter's assertions eventually rang true: The stockmen ended up with a sliding fee scale and people still suspect
and/or denounce the price of leasing the public lands as "subsidy." While the grazing fee moved slowly up to ten cents and
twelve cents per AUM, a movement was underway to base the
fee on fair-market value.[11] By 1958, fees were changed to reflect
this value. Former head of BLM and now a public-land policy
historian, Marion Clawson notes that the Forest Service had sup-
ported the move to fair-market value for many years, but neither
agency did anything about it because of opposition among livestock operators. By the 1960s the government was determined to
organize the fee structure and raise grazing fees. Studies on an
equitable way to estimate fees finally led to a fair market determination and a sliding grazing fee based on a formula: the costs of
running livestock on the grazing lands on BLM and Forest Service lands is subtracted from the average market value of forage
sold by states and individuals. Clawson notes that in 1966, by
the formula, the value of an AUM was $1.23 while the fee ac-
tually paid on the grazing districts was 33 cents/ AUM. In 1984,
the grazing fee by formula was $1.38, while one rancher said he

received $10.50 for some private, "market value"grazing.

The Taylor Grazing Act was up for reauthorization in 1985, and the year closed with no action being taken. Much of the debate and discussion surrounded the perceived subsidy of stockmen and of giving away the public range for less than market value. Wyoming congressman Richard Cheney introduced a bill that would not change the current formula for the grazing leases, but faces great opposition by environmentalists and other interests who would like to see an end to the "give away of the public's grass," as the argument goes. The debate over the reauthorization is anything but a mass public discussion. Fogged in the mist of budget battles, the only people really participating in the discussion are the special interests: the ranching groups and the environmentalists. After a year of debate, the bill has just begun to work its way slowly through the legislative maze, with discussion remaining centered upon the "fair-value" issues and the subsidies the grazing prices give ranchers.

Another question in the debate over the grazing fees will be the issue of subsidy and of subsidizing private parties using the publics' resources. A fair report of this issue must note, however, that the price per AUM is as pernicious a subsidy as is the federal subsidy to the timber industry or to the coal industry with the reduced prices received for the nation's renewable and non-renewable resources.

Along with the current discussion regarding a new definition of fair market value and value of use of the resource comes a new view of the history of grazing rights and incentives. The new economic view asserts that overgrazing was encouraged by the lack of reliable access to or use of the public grazing lands that served as common ground before the turn of the 20th century. "The existing arrangement of bureaucratically-assigned use privileges is not a satisfactory alternative to formal property rights," argues economist Gary Libecap. "Such privileges are necessarily unstable as the bureau adjusted them to meet changing political conditions. Further, formal grazing privileges assign rights to use the resources, but not to the resource itself, and that reduced the incentive of individuals to maximize the rental value of the range."

As the discussion turns to the controversy over use of the grazing lands, and what the value of that use should be, we can expect to hear much more from the camps that encourage private interest and private ownership of grazing lands — and thus personal responsibility for the continued health of the range. Questions remain, however: Is judicious use of the resource in private hands, relying upon efficient and positive self-interest more of a value to the public than potentially mediocre, but still publicly-owned, lands? Put simply, is it more important to us that the land be conserved and wisely used but under private ownership, or is it more important to us that we own the public lands and are willing to accept leasing them at less than market value or seeing them overgrazed?

Because the BLM lands are managed for multiple use, management of grazing is no longer the primary purpose of the agency, at least in terms of revenue enhancing. When the Dust Bowl was raging, making the obvious value of the public lands by all appearances nil, another set of public resources were becoming popular and vital. Beneath the grass lay vast resources of oil, gas, coal and other minerals that would build the our industrialized nation.

ENERGY AND MINERALS

Energy and mineral policy in the United States followed to some extent the legacy of western civilization: the sub-surface mineral wealth — early on considered to be only gold and silver — belonged to the King. In general in the United States, privately owned land also meant private ownership of the sub-surface minerals, with one caveat: If the land had been public domain and title had been transferred to a surface owner, the mineral rights remained with the government. Historian and former BLM Director Marion Clawson states that such "split-estates" were divided in the United States to a unsuspected degree.[12] Over 100 million acres in the U.S. that were once public domain are now in private hands, with the mineral titles retained by the United States government.

The rainless country was the last frontier, and in its poisoned areas, without dignity, the wayfaring Americans came to the end of their story. Reclamation is a shining image of something or other — aspiration, it may be, or futility. Confronted by the last acres of the tradition and finding them incapable of producing, the Americans wasted millions trying to enforce their will on the desert. The impulse and the glory of the migration died hard, but when the desert was conceded to be desert in spite of will-power, they died at last, in something between pathos and farce. So here ends ingloriously what began gloriously on the Atlantic littoral, below the falls line, and the last phase of the westward wayfaring has the appearance of a joke. Yet, this having always been a country of paradox, there is something more than a joke. Before that ending the Westerner learned something. Implicit in the westward surge, both a product and a condition of it, was the sentiment that has been called, none too accurately, the American Dream. It is a complex sentiment not too easily phrased.

The plain evidence of the frontier movement, from the falls line on, indicated that there could be no limit but the sky to what the Americans might do. The sublimate of our entire experience was just this: here was a swamp and look! Here is Chicago. Every decade of expansion, every new district that was opened, backed up the evidence till such an expectation was absolutely integral with the national progress.

There was no limit but the sky: American ingenuity, American will power, American energy could be stopped by nothing whatever but would go on forever building Chicagos. It was a dream that, in the nature of things, had to be wrecked on reality sometime, but in actual fact the West was the first point of impact. Just as the pioneer had to give up his ace and learn mechanics when he crossed the hundredth meridian, just as he had to abandon his traditional individualism, so he had to reconcile himself to the iron determinism he faced. In the arid country just so much is possible, and when that limit has been reached nothing more can be done. The West was industry's stepchild, but it set a boundary beyond which industrialism could not go. American ingenuity, will power, and energy were spectacular qualities, but against the fact of rainfall, they simply didn't count.

The mountains and high plains, which had seen the end of the frontier movement and had caused the collapse of the pioneer culture, thus also set the first full stop to the American dream. Of the Americans, it was the Westerners who first understood that there are other limits than the sky.

Bernard DeVoto
1934

Unlike the other natural resources of forests and grazing land, no public or federal government inventory has been taken of the mineral, oil, gas or coal wealth of the public lands. This task is left to the private sector's interest in exploration. The obvious result of this policy is that there is a lack of information about the perceived wealth and value of energy under public lands. Without public knowledge of the extent of resources and the value of that energy, how can a fair price be set? This method of letting the private companies keep the information has contributed to the perception that the public is not receiving fair value for the energy and mineral resources under the public lands, since the resource information is based on private industries' own figures. The other side of the argument is that the private company that takes the risk of exploration should receive the benefit of pay-off; market-value for the right to chance the risk would deter most companies from developing the nation's resources, to the detriment of everyone.

The Minerals Acts of 1866 and 1872 reflect that the mining of mineral wealth was the "most important, if not the only reasonable, use of the public lands," says Clawson.[13] "Since there was no explicit recognition given to other possible uses, the laws have enabled mineral claims to override many other claims for public lands." The 1872 Act provided for anyone to enter any unreserved public domain lands, and with evidence of a discovery (no matter how small), the acreage of land could be claimed for a nominal investment of 100 dollars, indicating a "serious" assessment of the potential resource.

With the discovery of oil shortly after the 1872 Act (by a rig on private land), a new era in public-land use dawned. The placer claims provided for in the 1872 Act did not appropriately fit the case of petroleum and gas; the law required discovery for a claim to be valid, but discovery of oil required some rights to drill in the first place. Between 1910 and 1920, the government began to close down lands that were suspected of having oil reserves and confusion reigned as to what exactly to do about oil, the extent of the U.S. petroleum reserves and their use. Few had foreseen the importance oil would play in both the U.S security internationally and as a revenue source for the government.[14] The years around the turn of the century also saw the discussion — and the eventual decision — that government should lease rather than sell land with mineral deposits; conversely, that government had the ability to refuse leases on lands.

This era marked another juncture in the management of the public lands. The development — and thus to some extent, the management — of the commodity now lay in the hands of private developers rather than the federal government. Private industry initiated interest in mining or exploring for resources, rather than the use and management of those resources being initiated solely by the government.

Due, in part, to the confusion brought about by interest in oil, the Mineral Leasing Act of 1920 was passed, which set up competitive and non-competitive leasing. Anyone may non-competitively lease a section of land for oil or gas exploration; the lease is then usually sold to a professional developer for one to two percent royalty from any resource produced. The government receives one-eighth of the value of production or an annual rental of one dollar per acre, unless royalties exceed that rent. Competitive leasing usually takes place where a known reservoir of oil or gas exists. Once oil is found in one block, perhaps through non-competitive leasing, then the rest of the block is put up for lease competitively, with a bid secured by a cash bonus. The 1920 Act also applies to oil shale, potash, phosphate, sodium and coal.

Throughout this time — and through today — there is no real policy or policy objective defined for use of the energy and mineral resources. Are we to use the resources today or reserve them for tomorrow? "Interior Department policy on mineral development on public lands seems to have been rather poorly defined, if not just confused," notes Clawson. "Conservation has been emphasized from time to time, although the term has not always been clearly defined. Sometimes it has meant avoiding waste in handling products; sometimes, avoiding an unduly rapid rate of oil extraction; and at other times, reserving minerals for later use. But, in spite of the schizophrenic policies regulating

mineral development, there has always been a great deal of
support for such endeavors, and, by and large, the Department
has been rather friendly to the mineral industry ."[15]

At the end of World War II, 5000 oil and gas leases were in
effect on the public lands. By the end of 1960, the number had
increased to 130,000. In 1983, 432 competitive leases were issued, with revenues of 29.4 million dollars received in bonus
bids. Three thousand fifty non-competitive bids were issued.
There were just over 110,000 energy-mineral leases in effect in
the western states as of 1982, with receipt of about 750 million
dollars accruing.

In addition to the public land leases, the Outer Continental
Shelf (OCS) was opened to oil leasing in 1953, when President
Eisenhower signed the "tidelands bill" that gave states title to the
acres of land below sea level, below the average tide line three
miles from shore. The International Law of the Sea would increase the acreage to 20 to 200 miles out, depending on the area.
The price of leases for the OCS lands is an average of 1000 dollars. More than 560 million acres (total U.S.) are leased. The
Outer Continental Shelf leases have contributed over 50 billion
dollars to the U.S. treasury since they were first leased in 1953;
the revenue from the OCS leases is seven times the revenues received from on-shore leases.

The balance between energy — the largest money-maker for
the BLM — and grazing is only part of the issue concerning policy and use of the public lands. Wildlife management, recreation,
watershed maintenance and/or preservation will begin to take a
larger share of BLM's concentration in the future. A brief run-
down of the questions we can expect to face in deciding how we
want to use the ranges of the west follows.

Recreation   Until recently, the idea of recreating on the range
lands was a little this side of bizarre. Why go to what are considered to be the leftovers of the American west when the parks
and national forests are so readily available? Even Clawson, a
former director of BLM, noted that the lands were "drab" or, in
the case of Alaska, basically inaccessible. Yet, in 1984, there

were some 52 million visits to the lands and recreational areas.
The major form of recreation during these visits was something
the BLM calls "motorized recreation," be it off-road vehicles,
such as dirt bikes or dune buggies, or "driving for pleasure . . .
The primary purpose of the riding or driving, train or bus tour-
ing, is for recreation." The second type of recreation does not
include interstate highway traffic or sightseeing, the BLM guide
says. A prime example is in California where 23,000 visitor
hours were spent in the dunes and desert dirt biking and dune
buggy riding in 1983. The question arises as to whether the value of such recreational use merits a higher fee for use than exists
at present to help pay for the restoration and management of the
areas. The BLM figures that each visitor paid an average of two
cents per hour, or 41 cents per visit in 1983. Are people willing
to pay more for the reclamation required just as a result of their
recreating as private energy companies are required to pay for
their use and reclamation of the land?

Coal The controversy generated over coal leasing in 1982 and
1983 under the James Watt administration of the Department of
Interior is a good example of the tenor of the issues facing BLM
and the range lands. Congress ordered a halt to coal leasing during Watt's last year in office because, it charged, the leasing was
not bringing anything close to fair-market value for a one-time
use resource such as coal. Opponents to the leasing charged that
the proposed sales of the coal, the largest in the history of BLM,
were a "give-away." They said that the sales would simultaneously flood the market, lowering the price across the market,
and gyp future energy resources since these were being sold at
"bargain basement" prices. The coal industry countered that the
prices being bid — an average of three and a half cents per ton
— were, in fact, fair prices. They added that if they didn't secure
the leases, the energy stability of the industry in the future and
thus of the country would be at stake, since it takes some 15
years to bring a coal mine on line and into production. Two investigations were conducted into the least offering with the GAO
finally charging that the Watt Administration had shortchanged

the U.S. treasury — and thus the people of the U.S. — 100
million dollars in 1982, through questionable, non-competitive
lease sales.

Commencement of the coal leasing program is expected to
occur again by the late 1980s, after internal investigations into
the lease sales are finished. Some groups tried to have the entire
coal program reconsidered — and thus the levels that were being
offered — by requiring that new environmental impact statements be developed for the sale areas. It was argued that watershed protection was not taken into account. It was also noted
that, because of split-estate rights, ranchers needed to use of the
range surface lands that would be removed by strip mines to get
at the coal.

For BLM, the universal question raised and still unan-
swered is the priority of energy development over the other uses
of the range: at what price are we willing to have a non-
renewable, one-time use resource mined while in the process, the
land is closed to other uses? The question also reverts to a more
fundamental question regarding all of our natural resources:
What is the true value, and thus price, of use?

ELIZABETH DARBY JUNKIN

DENALI NATIONAL PARK, ALASKA

IV. Alaska

Alaska — the "Great Land" in Aleutian. The name itself conjures up a thousand pictures to each of us: Denali National Park, Mt. McKinley, Glacier Bay. Whether or not we each ever see the Great Land in reality, we share a portrait of it that is colored with a perception of wildness about the land and a sense of its incredible size. The land appears in our minds as it is in reality: A vast, wild land that throws the scale of the United States off kilter if we try to categorize Alaska as but another of the 50 states of the Union.

In terms of area, Alaska's 365 million acres make it two times the size of Texas. If you place the Alaska panhandle on Savannah, Georgia, the Aleutian Islands would extend to Los Angeles and the northern boundary would rest on our continental border with Canada. Alaska's coastline is 35,000 miles; that's a distance equal to driving from San Diego to Seattle 35 times, or driving from Portland, Maine to Miami 19 times. As a peninsula, Alaska is the largest in the Western Hemisphere. It is the only state in the country in which entire ecosystems have been set aside in wildlife refuge, national park and wilderness form. Denali National Park and Preserve, as an example, is 5.7 million acres or about 8900 square miles and is just a little larger than the state of Massachusetts. It is estimated that 160,000 acres of Alaska — about 1/20 of a percent of the state — has been "cleared, built on or otherwise directly altered by man through settlement or resource development."[1]

In sheer magnitude and in its effect upon the human spirit, Alaska is a different country. It is possibly more foreign to our understanding than the western frontier was, where living with extremes was commonplace. Nineteenth century settlers found a frontier that was incomprehensible in size and demands. They

were confronted with a foreign land of extremes of plenty and
hunger, extremes in vulnerability to the wild weather of the west,
extremes in that an individual's decision meant survival or death.
Alaska is as incomprehensible today to 20th century man, despite
his advantage of having technology that makes what was impas-
sable wilderness passable with a minimum of trouble or hazard.
To 20th century man, Alaska has represented a frontier not unlike that which faced our earlier generations of homesteaders and
explorers in this country. Previous to 1980, it represented an opportunity to see if an individual still had within him or her the
mettle that the settlers of the west had both in mind and body,
when facing the western 11 states during the 1800s.

Yet, Alaska also represents the ultimate test of Americans'
ability to engage in the making of land policy — of our ability to
manage ourselves — because the land is not indestructible. To an
extent that far exceeds any previous time in history, the future of
Alaska's lands is dependent upon our wisdom of action and our
understanding of our choices in using the land. As Rod Nash
wrote in *Wilderness and the American Mind*[2]:

*"It was said continually that Alaska was America's last frontier. Some
hoped this meant opportunity for settlement and development as had
been the rule on earlier American Frontiers. Others relished the idea of
Alaska as a permanent frontier where Americans could visit their past
both in person and as an idea. 'Armchair' tourists, intellectual import-
ers of Alaska's wilderness, were among the most vocal in defending land
they never expected to see. They said that Alaska represented the nation's last chance to do things right the first time."*

To an important extent, the same psychological mix among
state residents and lower "48-ers" is associated with Alaska today, five years after the signing of the Alaska National Interest
Lands Act of 1980, which designated some 131 million acres of
parks, refuges and wilderness in Alaska. While Washington
D.C., landlord of 73 percent of the state, considers Alaska land
policy to essentially be a closed book, state residents, developers
and conservationists see many a battle yet to be fought over
Alaska's wild lands. As we shall see later in this chapter, the
perceptions of abundant frontier, of a chance to "do it right" and

of the idea that the issues have essentially already been decided, are all right — and wrong.

Although Alaska was purchased by the United States in 1867, it was largely ignored by the federal government until some 30 years ago. That is not to say that this land of vast resources sat empty for 90 years, but that life went on there as it had essentially for the previous 500 years — with a native population relying on the land to provide home and a habitat for wildlife that provided their necessities and sustenance. As a people, the Alaska native lived separately, basically ignoring or working with non-native settlers. Again, it was a situation reminiscent of the early French fur trappers who lived in the American West in the late 1700s and early 1800s. The recognition of this native population when the federal government began to take an interest in Alaska, starting with statehood in 1958, and later in 1971, opened a new chapter in the history of land settlement, wilderness, frontier philosophy, and in a land ethic. It simultaneously closed forever the book on government-sponsored conquering of the frontier. As Nash observes, wilderness, as a value in man's mind, "had come of age."[3]

With statehood, a different sort of battle began on the frontier. It was the battle in earnest for what some writers of the time called the "heart and soul" of Alaska. Prior to 1958 and statehood, 99.8 percent of the state was "federally owned," use and ownership by the 60,000 natives notwithstanding. The state was allotted 104 million acres for their selection. As a response to being ignored, in attitude if not in fact, the Allied Federation of Natives claimed half of the state in 1966, their rights to the land having been perfected with thousands of years of use. Interior Secretary Stuart Udall suspended all land transfers until the native claims could be resolved by Congress. His action quieted the din resulting from private parties, industry and the state readying to compete for land titles.

The discovery of oil on the North Slope in 1968 added pressure to the pressure cooker. A compromise was struck with the natives in 1971: the United States gave them 44 million acres of land to be chosen from a pool of 117 million acres and one billion dollars, in exchange for all of their other aboriginal claims to

The Congress finds and declares that — the continuation of the opportunity for subsistence uses by rural residents of Alaska, including both Natives and non-Natives, on the public lands . . . is essential to Native physical, economic, traditional and cultural existence and to non-Native physical, economic, traditional and social existence."

Alaska Lands Act
1980

the land. The compromise also gave them political recognition. The natives were to form twelve native-owned, profit-making corporations as part of the Alaska Native Claims Settlement Act (ANCSA) of 1971. With one-third of the state allocated to the native population, the battle continued for the other two-thirds. The state immediately filed a request to select an additional 77 million acres just before signing of the ANCSA agreement; Interior Secretary Rogers Morton refused to recognize the state's request. ANCSA made it clear that no other land claims would be recognized until Section 17(d)(2) of the act was satisfied: designation of "National Interest Lands" by Congress. ANCSA gave Congress until December 18, 1978 to designate which lands "were vital to the national interest" as well as to Alaska's interest. Central to the discussion of a definition of these lands was what people came to call "the setting aside of more Yellowstones."

In the debate over designation and purpose of the Alaska National Interest Lands, old strains of the arguments on wilderness reemerged. It was argued that man could never subjugate a land so far away, or so wild — both in terms of wilderness and climate. The perception was of a frontier, abundant as much with wildlife and resources as it was with possibility. It was a perception that recalled the attitude toward Yellowstone in 1872.

To the writers and explorers who set Yellowstone aside 113 years ago, it was inconceivable that there would be anything like the traffic jams that fill Yellowstone's roads today during the summer season. The place was a frontier that was in the midst of wilderness, promising the courageous visitor adventure or peril, depending upon his perspective. Yet, with development of the West being encouraged, Yellowstone was set aside as a natural wonder that remains today.

The same was argued for Alaska: Who was to say that the same influx of interest and people could not or would not occur in Alaska? It was simply the advent of better transportation that opened the west, making the wilds of Yellowstone a mere few days' drive from anywhere in the country. How could any of us predict how our accessibility to Alaska would affect the wildlands and the perception of the frontier that Alaska represented?

A little under a million people travelled to Alaska last year to visit. Historically, the number of tourists visiting the state grows between 6 and 15 percent per year. This means that the number of tourists visiting the state — with commensurate backcountry use — doubles every seven years. The 20th century armchair tourists and would-be frontiersmen argued that the bush plane, used with as much commonality and frequency as the pick-up truck is throughout the west, represented just the kind of easy-access that would conquer the frontier. Perhaps, as Nash argues, Alaska is relatively smaller and less isolated than Yellowstone was at the time it was set aside. Although a person can sit in the middle of some of the wildest wilderness land there is today in Alaska, it is rare not to hear a small plane passing overhead.

Similar arguments were made about the seeming abundance of fish and wildlife in Alaska as in the lower-48 western wilderness of earlier.There was enough to go around in this land of plenty. It has been argued since, the only reason there seemed to be a wealth of wildlife in Alaska was because there were simply fewer people in the state. In reality, Alaska has less of a population of fish and game than Oregon, according to a varied list of biologists.[4] This assertion remains a point of contention among local Alaskans, as they deal with the issue of whom should continue to be allowed to subsistence hunt and fish on the National Interest Lands. The argument still rages today.

Alaska did not have to contend with other pressures the western frontier faced: homesteaders seeking large parcels of land for farms and ranches. The lack of interest in large-scale use of the land for agriculture is a result of the state's location and has served to effectively remove large portions of the tundra from the kinds of uses and abuses that brought death and drouth to the grass lands of the west. The growing season in Alaska is only 45 days throughout the tundra areas. Most environmental impact statements report that there is simply less resilience of this kind of soil in the ecosystems of Alaska. Opponents to the setting aside of large parcels of Alaska argued that the weather alone would protect this land and that neither nature nor the state needed any help from the federal government in preserving the bulk of the land as frontier.

The process of identifying lands "vital to the national interest" wore on through the eight years Congress had to identify the lands. Interior Secretary Rogers Morton recommended in 1973, 83 million acres for permanent federal management, but action was delayed on the recommendation due to the nation's preoccupation with Watergate. When Jimmy Carter took office in 1976, there was but two years left for the lands to be designated before the ANSCA deadline after which the country would be opened to free entry by private parties and business. The vision of reenacting the largest land rush in the history of the United States pressed Congress to action.

In May, 1978, Representative Morris Udall introduced House Bill 39 that would have set aside some 124 million acres in national parks, refuges and wilderness areas in Alaska. Alaska Governor Jay Hammond requested that the acreage be reduced to 25 million acres and called for a federal-state partnership for management of the land. Hammond reasoned that if the typical national park standards were lowered and the required standards for use of the land by state and private parties raised, that more of the land would retain its wild character. He pointed to examples like Yellowstone in the "lower 48" where developers pointed to the pristine requirements within the park system as fair exchange for their development excesses. His proposal fell upon deaf ears. The interview with Governor Hammond addresses this point in Chapter 3.

"House Bill 39 poses an opportunity of historic dimensions," Udall told the House during debate. "As long as any of us serves in this House, we shall vote on no more vital, more far-reaching, more memorable conservation measure . . . this will indeed be the land and wildlife vote of the century."[5]

Udall's legislation passed the House, but the Senate threatened filibuster through the efforts of Alaska Senator Mike Gravel. By November 1978, it was apparent that the ANCSA deadline would not be met, and private interests were lining up at the border for a land rush not seen in 150 years. On November 16, 1978, Interior Secretary Cecil Andrus withdrew 110 million acres from mineral entry and state selection. The Secretary can close or open public domain lands to entry, as it falls under his powers of management. President Carter on December 1, 1978, using the weapon of executive power similarly exercised 80 years earlier by Theodore Roosevelt through the Antiquities Act of 1906, set aside 56 million acres of land in Alaska in a national monument. He directed the Department of Interior to withdraw another 40 million acres for a wildlife refuge and he directed the Department of Agriculture to remove 11 million acres from mineral entry. Carter's actions mirrored Roosevelt's early actions in removing some of the public lands from private entry, both in result and in the people's response to such bold, unilateral steps taken by executive authority for preservation. Carter's moves, however, were only stop-gap and could be reversed by similar executive order; they were meant to hold the tide of land-seekers until Congress could pass an Alaska lands bill.

Udall started another bill through Congress, with the help of Ohio Congressman John Seiberling, but by this time, every conceivable party was involved in the fray over the land. The Alaska Coalition was established — a coalition of interest groups and associations whose membership cut laterally and vertically across the landscape of special interests — in favor of an Alaska lands bill. "America will never see a buffalo herd again," Udall told Congress during debate for the vote on his second bill. "And if we are not wise today, our grandchildren will not be able to see a caribou herd. This is the test of our Congressional careers. This may be the most important vote we cast."

The House passed the bill, which designated 127.5 million acres of National Interest Lands, including 67.5 million acres of designated wilderness. The area set aside was about the size of all of the Pacific Coast states. The Senate, however, offered an alternative bill, with less acreage. The House refused to compromise, until an event occurred outside the process and outside of the debate on Alaska, an event that changed the context of the discussion over the amount of land: Reagan's election. Ronald Reagan's election to the presidency in 1980 brought with it an accompanying change in attitude toward federal involvement in states' matters, and it brought a different definition of conservation that emphasized use of the public lands. With the change

*N*ewton Drury, when he was *Director of the National Park Service, said: "Surely the great United States of America is not so poor we cannot afford to have these places, nor so rich that we can do without them."*

When all the nonrenewable resources have been dug up, hauled away, piped away, to satisfy the needs of a cert-ain span of users, Alaska can still have a renewable, self-perpetuating resources of inestimable value — value eco-nomical, value spirtual, value for the health of the people.

We cannot foretell the future, but we can give a nod toward it by putting this last treasure of wild country into an interest-bearing savings account.

In the long view — all Alaska needs to do is be Alaska.

Margaret Murie
Testifying in favor of the
Alaska Lands Act, 1980.

in administrations, the House accepted the Senate bill,with Udall even today saying that the bill "accomplished 90 percent of its objective."[6]

President Carter signed the Alaska National Interest Lands Conservation Act on December 2, 1980, setting aside a total of 104 million acres as National Interest Lands. The bill revoked the stop-gap creation of the national monuments Carter had set aside two years earlier. With the bill, the state received 105 million acres and the natives had their claim to 44 million acres for hunting and living needs confirmed. The bill guaranteed that oil and gas exploration and drilling could take place on 95 percent of the Alaska mainland and in 100 percent of the off-shore areas.

Of the 28 percent of the state set aside as National Interest Lands, 56.7 million acres were put into the National Wilderness Preservation System. Wilderness, however, received a different working definition than in the "lower 48," as did the protections accompanying national park designation: hunting, trapping and timbering on a subsistence basis is allowed in the national park and wilderness areas in Alaska by those who qualify under the standards of relying upon the land for subsistence. Access to and through the "wilderness" using airplanes, motorboats and snow-mobiles, where such use can be proven to be "traditional," is also permitted, but is basically disallowed in practice. The category of "subsistence users" includes all natives and residents of many local areas around the state, ranging from rural politicians and private businessmen to locals with little income.

The National Park System received 43.6 million acres, doubling the size of the entire U.S. National Park System. Twenty-six new wild and scenic rivers were added, along with ten new national parks and monuments and adjustments to three other parks. A system of "Wildlife Preserves" was set up, which are located adjacent to the national parks. Sport hunting by anyone is allowed in these "preserves."

Present and Future Issues

The largest mining industry in the state is sand and gravel, although other minerals have been located. U.S. Borax identified

one of the largest molybdenum deposits in the world near Ketchi-
kan, but depression in the moly market has limited the production. The project has estimated that production will be ended in
1987. Gold is the second largest mining industry in the state,
bringing in revenues of 70 million dollars in 1985.[7]

Alaska is believed to have about half of the United States'
total resources of coal. Geologists estimate that perhaps 80 percent of that reserve underlies the 23 million acre National Petroleum Reserve in the North Slope. Production of coal is only taking place presently at the Usibelli Mine near Healy. As with all
the other potential natural resource uses, such as timber, the cost
of transportation prohibits large-scale development.

The timber cutting in the Tongass National Forest is one of
the most controversial uses of the public's natural resources.
Large-scale timber cutting of Sitka spruce in the southeastern
coast area continues only because of subsidies from the U.S.
government. The U.S. public pays in subsidies 95 cents of the
dollar made from the sale of the wood pulp to the Far East.[8] The
high cost of transportation makes Alaska's natural resources un-
competitive in both United States and international markets.

The same is true for coal production, as well as the oil and
gas that is mined from the North Slope. The oil and gas reserves
in Prudhoe Bay alone provide about 18 percent of total U.S. production, with the once-controversial-now-accepted pipeline providing shipment of some 1.5 million barrels per day from the
North Slope to the port at Valdez. Estimates indicate that in
1983, one-third of the reserve had been pumped and the companies involved were about to undertake a massive water flood to
keep up production.[9]

The extent to which Alaska plans to continue to develop its
natural resources is the main issue on the horizon. Whether subsidies — federal or state — will lower the cost of the natural resources so that development can take place is only part of the
question facing Alaska. Tourism is the third largest source of revenue for the state after oil and gas and commercial fishing, re-
spectively. Does the state want to develop its resources when it is
the beauty of the wilderness and nature itself that brings the tourists? As Governor Jay Hammond has pointed out, the high

wealth days of oil and gas revenues are drawing to a close and
the state is casting about looking for new sources of revenue.
These questions of choice will become crucial over the next ten
years. How do state residents want to use its resources? And,
just as importantly, how do the American people want to balance
the use with setting aside the resources of the public lands in
Alaska? There is still time to make a choice in Alaska and the
impact will be greater than is still possible in the American West.

One issue rising on the immediate horizon is in Arctic National Wildlife Refuge, which comes up for wilderness recommendation in 1986. The refuge is suspected to have vast resources of
oil and gas, being adjacent to Barrow and the Arctic Ocean. It is
also the only remaining U.S. area that qualifies for wilderness
designation within the Arctic Circle. Congress will be undertaking the debate during 1986 about whether the Arctic National
Wildlife Range will remain multiple use, with the associated energy and mineral availability, or whether we should set aside this
wildlife refuge as wilderness.

The Bureau of Land Management had jurisdiction over most
of Alaska before the land claims acts were settled. The agency is
still dealing with the state's selection of state lands and the selection process is one of the issues facing Alaska in years to come.
As an example, the state would like to choose lands adjacent to
the Hall road. It runs along the pipeline and very close to Gates
of the Arctic National Park, which is at present only accessible
by charter plane. Choosing that land would do much to open up
the interior of the state to easy access and more development.
This presents a question for Alaska's future. How much development is good? Is the frontier mentality — of opening the state
and assuming that all of man's development in the state is necessarily a boon — a goal? Or is there more value for the state in
keeping large segments in a wild, hard-to-access form? What is
the ambiance and the lifestyle Alaskans want and how does that
affect the rest of the American peoples' vision   for Alaska?

Another issue facing the management of all of the public
lands in Alaska surrounds the ANCSA. In 1991, the native
corporation shares that were part of the settlement with natives in
1971 can be sold to non-natives. At the same time, the shares

will become subject to federal taxes. In some cases, the shares will have to be sold to pay for the taxes. In other cases, selling of these shares will be hard not to do; at a recent hearing on the 1991 matter, some natives testified that they had been offered sums as large as 3.5 million dollars for a 160 acre lake-front allotment of land. The land allotments that the natives hold, as part of their traditional rights in Alaska, are located throughout the state, in national parks, preserves and wilderness areas. Selling of these parcels of land will open these areas to private development in a way that potentially and effectively circumvents the purpose of national park and wilderness protections. The question arises concerning the value of these protections; the threat of development causes one to wonder whether Congress would want to — or even can — go back and reinstate in Alaska more stringent protections that accompany national park and wilderness designation in the "lower 48"? It becomes a question of what price wildness? What is the value in setting aside a land where the frontier-feeling survives, simply for the value of knowing the frontier is there to challenge is each in our own way and in our own time?

The issues facing Alaska in the coming years are similar to those that accompanied the development of the frontier in the "lower 48," and yet by sheer size and magnitude of the land that will be effected, the issues will be uniquely Alaskan. It has been argued that the wild and untouched Alaska offers us a chance to look at ourselves and to see how each of us measure up to the past challenges which contributed to the making of our American character as we settled this country. Travelling through Alaska, one is constantly challenged with trying to comprehend a land so large, where nature simply functions as it has for thousands of years and where we can witness our own importance, equally our unimportance, and our place in this world. We perceive ourselves as separate from the wild land, yet see no more clearly than when in the midst of it, that our world would not exist without this foundation of resources. It could also be argued that Alaska, wild, offers a chance for us to challenge ourselves with the future — still — for in making these decisions, we form our own history for those yet to come.

DEATH VALLEY NATIONAL MONUMENT, CALIFORNIA

CHAPTER 3

THE VOICES

What follows is sort of an open forum/policy discussion on paper. The voices, speaking on what the value of public lands are and what the purpose of the lands might be, are the result of formal and informal conversation with people — real people who happen to be policy makers, leaders, special interest representatives, ranchers, people who use the land. People were asked the questions noted here and asked to respond from any perspective he or she wished — as policy maker or rancher, or both, for example. Conversation followed to probe the person's attitudes and feelings about land policy, the public lands, management and primary use. These are the guide-line questions that were asked:

•What is the value of the public lands of the American West? How would we describe this value to those who may not ever see them?

•What is the purpose of still maintaining lands that are publicly owned?

•What should we look to the public lands to provide now and in the future?

•If we were to look a hundred years into the future, what would be the picture you would like to see of these lands? What is your vision for them? Describe it physically, as if a painting or a photograph. What would you change from today's picture that you have?

•From that point a hundred years into the future, let's look back at us, today, as historians might eventually look at us and our society. How would you assess our management of our public lands and our natural resources today if you were looking back from a point in the future? What would you change?

As we read through these responses, we might consider our own answers to the questions posed, and assess what the future value of the lands might be to each of us and to our children's children.

MORRIS UDALL   ————————————————————

Representative Morris Udall, (Dem-Arizona) is a legend in environmental policy circles. He led the battle on the 1980 Alaska National Interest Lands Act. He has chaired the Interior Committee since 1977 and according to the National Journal, has always been counted as a friend, but not an automatic vote, by environmentalists.

JUNKIN: How can I describe the value of these public lands — Alaska, and the other public lands in the western United States? How do we ascertain what they are worth?

UDALL: Well, I think you have to take a very broad view. There are so many things that they hold. The multi-use concept is involved in this kind of description. You look out of your airplane and there is a forest a hundred miles long and it produces the water supply for people. It produces timber. It has minerals. It has recreation. It has a wilderness component; it is just a whole range of things. It is kind of the nest from which much good, much that is essential to our life, comes.

J: So both the tangible and the intangible worth are there?

U: Yes, all those qualities all wrapped up together. That's why this Sagebrush Rebellion was always misbegotten and inappropriate. The people never saw what the land was trying to do. These were — in their simplistic view — wastelands, or lands that were not really developed in America. Why didn't we get on with this exploitation and put it in private hands and let people get their bulldozers and build things, and subjugate the land.

J: I'd like to try to look at a couple of historical questions. One is history looking forward, if that's possible. Thomas Jefferson had incredible vision, I personally think, just in looking at the Louisiana Purchase. It was wild and inaccessible, totally useless by standards of the day, and yet he used up more money than we had in the treasury at the time to purchase it. If you and I look a

A nd I would like to think that was my guiding story in Alaska in the Alaska Lands Bill. I wanted people to say a hundred years from now, "Gee, it was great that some people had the sense and vision to say here, out in the huge land, how fortunate we are to have 375,000 acres of land owned by the people. There were people that had enough sense to set it aside so that future generations, all down the future time, could enjoy and share in its resources and its benefits." It isn't a one time exploitation, it's a huge right, it's renewed and it's there as long as we have the species on the planet.

Representative Morris Udall

hundred years into the future right now, what is the view that you would like to have of the public lands? What, is the mental picture you would like to hold of it — and in that intangible way, what is the vision you see for them?

U: Well, that's the one sense that man has over the other animals: if you can have vision, you can think ahead and plan ahead. I don't know any other part of nature, any species that has that ability. And I think you have got to focus. You have got to be a fierce watchdog of the future. The oath in the City of Athens where you would at least swear to transmit our city in as good a condition or better than we got it from the last generation — you have to think of it in those terms, rather than their [the lands] exploitation for our generation. And I would like to think that was my guiding story in Alaska in the Alaska Land Bill. I wanted people to say a hundred years from now, "Gee, it was great that some people had the sense and vision to say here, out in the huge land, how fortunate we are to have 375,000 acres of land owned by the people. There were people that had enough sense to set it aside so that future generations, all down the future time, could enjoy and share in its resources and its benefits." It isn't a one-time exploitation, it's a huge right, it's renewed and it's there as long as we have the species on the planet.

J: Are you saying that you want the public lands to remain status quo, as they are now . . .?

U: Yeah. That was one of the significant things we did with the BLM lands and the FLPMA [Federal Land Policy and Management Act] in the 1976 legislation. I was on the Public Land Law Review Commission which took five or six years in the sixties to sort out public lands and what we were doing with them. The first recommendation we made was to reverse the Taylor Grazing Act in the 1930s, which was a charter for public lands. [In it] Public lands were viewed as something that was temporarily in federal hands and should be gotten rid of and privatized, as soon as possible . . . that was the goal. You administered the lands with the major goal of getting rid of them.

The first recommendation the Public Land Law Review made, and the first finding, was that they ought to be kept. And how many countries . . . You look around the world — how many countries would wish and hope that they had had that kind of vision — the Germans, the French? They don't have wilderness or forests that amount to much, and they should have had that vision so say "This is a resource, and it's not a bad idea to have large chunks of land in public hands. It's a good idea."

J: What are the questions that the public at large should be asking themselves — to see that the lands are being used right?

U: The question is, are they being preserved or managed so that the benefit will be there for others? I mean, that is the answer to the fundamental question.

J: You were greatly involved in the Alaska Lands Act. Alaska seems to be at the point that the rest of the west was a hundred years ago . . .

U: And we have enough vision to make a different choice. Theodore Roosevelt saved us — because they were chopping up the timber in Minnesota, or Wisconsin, or some of those states. We forget that those states were covered by timber from one end of the state to the other. These robber barons went through that and left behind a sad legacy, and they were starting to do that in Alaska and we headed them off.

J: Do you think that's going to head it off productively for basically the duration of our generation?

U: Yeah, I think so. I think the protection will be stronger not only in Alaska, but down here. "What the hell is land grab. Why is the federal government taking over this and setting it aside and who needs all of these parks and wilderness areas," was what people were saying in the country. I think that kind of sentiment has half the strength that it had ten years ago. You can't find but a few right-wing-ultra-conservative-nuts around here in the House and Senate, who really are going to stand up and say, " We don't need to live with this" or "We don't need Alaska land. We should give away some more Alaska land." You don't find that sentiment. You did — it was very prevalent ten years ago.

J: So, it looks like maybe what we've got today will be what we might have 75 years from now?

U: Yeah, if we are lucky, and we may get a little bit more. Nobody's out buying up new chunks of federal land, but we still have the BLM Wilderness Review to go through, and we will get several million acres more in wilderness status — which is very important in terms of watershed and wildlife.

February 1985
Washington, D.C.

MALCOLM WALLOP ⎯⎯⎯⎯⎯⎯⎯⎯⎯⎯⎯⎯

Senator Malcolm Wallop (Republican, Wyoming) is currently Majority Whip in the Senate. He chairs the Senate Sub-Committee on Public Lands , Reserved Water and Resource Conservation. He has the added perspective of being a rancher and is a believer in the free market as an allocator of resources.

JUNKIN: The value of the public lands: how do we assess their value — tangible or intangible values? How would you describe them?

WALLOP: Clearly, they have both tangible and intangible values. That is, the intangible values will always shift. It is a matter of perception of the public, whoever that happens to be who is thinking about it at the moment, in the time that it is there. But however it shifts, it will always remain high. Whether it is for open space, for resources, or for wildlife, whether it is for a combination, or whether it is for national security — those things, you know it will always be there.

The tangible value also shifts. Much depends, for example, from the perspective of pricing, on the relative value of that commodity in the market place. Tangible value also shifts with relative value of minerals, with relative values of timber, and with relative accessibility of recreation and with public attitudes towards recreation. Because there was a time in this country when there were not many resources available outside the country. I suspect there may come a time again when that is the case, and so the tangible value would depend on the set of circumstances.

But there is another value, which I don't think many people recognize. That is the ability of the resources on the public lands to leaven the cost structure of any given thing. I'll put it this way: if there was nothing but private coal in the country, you could have an entirely different economic circumstance and you can see that government is keeping enough coal out there, leased to people who can make money on it at a lower price, outside the privately held resources. The same thing is in part true with grass, and part true of timber and other resources. I think it's true in terms of the recreation resource to a certain extent; what you can get from the private sector offerings is leavened by what is available in the public lands resource.

J: Is there one of these purposes of the public lands that takes precedence over the others?

W: No. Absolutely not. I think that is the worst of all possible worlds, because no matter which one or combination of ones that you would select you will always end up with a major distortion when government says, "People love it for this reason." And people don't. When you try to force rather than accommodate changing sensibilities, you end up with distortions that are terribly difficult to extract yourself from.

J: Then how could we define the "best use?" Or could we?

W: I don't think you've got one. I think it is a mistake to define the best use. And say that that's going to be it for the next hundred years. The "best use" is the appropriate management of it for the changing requirements of an advancing society, and they will change.

J: Two historical questions: one is looking historically into the future. And I wonder, what is the view that you have of the public land. What's your vision as you look out over Wyoming or Colorado, or over any of the western 13 states. What would you want to see a hundred years from now?

W: Something very similar to what we have today. A variety of options weighed in balance with each other, managed wisely, trying continually to hold this resource in a state of high value, recognizing that is going to change in certain ways. I think their value is that they are public lands. Public resources. And that's not to put myself in the camp that says we either ought to have millions of acres more because that's good value there, or in the camp that say that everything we have has irretrievable value to it. There clearly are judgments that should be made, but the great bulk of it, I think, has as its intrinsic value its very public nature.

J: And if we were to stand a hundred years in the future and look back at our generation today, how would you assess public land policy? What would you change?

W: Let's simplify it so that the land managers can spend more time managing the land and less time accommodating the ports, empowered by Congress, and a variety of things. I think you would have much, much more creative, well-managed from the standpoint of the environment and from the standpoint of development. You know we are in a navel-gazing status right now, and we make studies upon studies to find out what studies have already told us to reject something that we have already rejected.

I think it is a mistake to define the "best use." and say that that's going to be it for the next hundred years. The best use is the appropriate management of it for the changing requirements of an advancing society, and they will change.

Senator Malcolm Wallop

I think that it is good and wise for us to care about the lands deeply. I think it is not so good and wise of us in our caring to manage them to keep ourselves in offices under papers instead of out on the land itself, doing what good managers can do.

J: Are there questions that the great public out there should be asking themselves regarding the management of those lands?

W: I think there are. Because one of the single questions that recurs is that, in our powerful desires to preserve some things, we overlook certain other things which are real, I think. A valid question is, "Who would name any portion of ground anywhere in America and say that the inventory of living things was complete?" But you can find zillions of people who will tell you that the inventory of mineral things is complete. And that doesn't strike me as being a consistent view of management. And so I basically want one who would say that you always manage it for a future use, during the development of a single phase of it. Whether it is a recreational phase or a mineral development phase, or a timber harvesting phase, or grazing or a combination of them, you always manage it with the eye towards that point when this set of plans has been completed, that you will still have a tangible, visible, valuable asset. That is the thing that sustains its intangible value. So that if you manage anything just for today, from whatever perspective, whether it is wilderness or oil and gas development, or any of the other things we do on the land, if you manage it only from that perspective, you will soon find that you have done harm.

We are not in a world that sustains itself without being touched, and we have surrounded it. What is done in other places has an effect on our world, whether we do it or not. My hope and view would always be that whatever was going on, you would look at what the possibilities would be at the conclusion of the cycle.

February 1985
Washington D.C.

JOHN BADEN ⎯⎯⎯⎯⎯⎯⎯⎯⎯⎯⎯⎯⎯⎯⎯⎯⎯⎯⎯⎯

John Baden is director of the Political Economy Research Center in Bozeman, Montana. It is PERC, as the center is known, that is referred to by many other voices, as the people "who want to sell off all of the public lands and place them in private hands." It may sound a lot like the philosophy James Watt espoused while Secretary of the Interior, but that is a similarity which makes Baden cringe. While this misconception is oversimplified at least, and a misstatement at best, it is the result of economic arguments that are taken out of context and misunderstood by the media. The view of Baden and PERC represents one of the new directions of thought about public land management and policies. Unlike most of the other public land policies and philosophies today, Baden's philosophy is a product of the late 20th century. This view is one of the most controversial, new ideas in public land management.

BADEN: The context of American public lands is historical and philosophical. And for me it is very important to begin in 1776. There are two great documents in 1776 that I know of: obviously the first is the book, *The Wealth of Nations,* by Adam Smith, which is an extraordinarily powerful and important book. Smith was a genius and note that he was not an economist, he was a moral philosopher. The other great document, of course, was the Declaration of Independence.

Well, for a variety of reasons, the Articles of Confederation did not work well. There were some structural problems there, and so what happened in Philadelphia, in 1887, was that we came up with the U.S. Constitution. The U.S. Constitution is probably the most important document ever written; it is important in that for the very first time people sat down and consciously attempted to design a system that would produce an environment conducive to individual liberty and economic progress. And they understood, as evidenced by *The Federal Papers,* the basic lessons of *The Wealth of Nations* — and that is fundamentally that individuals are the best judge. They provide the best judgement of their own well-being. And they understood that power is used to disadvantage by those who don't have it; and they understood it throughout almost all of history: Government has been used as an engine of plunder. The government is, in fact, the most efficient engine of plunder ever designed because it holds down violence — people do not waste time, very much time, fighting and engaging in defensive activities, because the government provides a system, a context of law and order. Even a repressive and totalitarian government does that — enables people to get on with productivity and then, of course, takes a big chunk of it from them.

Our constitution was explicitly designed to make government and the use of government difficult and uncertain and expensive. So reliance for organizing the economy was placed upon individuals, offered in the context of courts, to adjudicate conflict in which government protects property rights. Individuals were then faced with strong incentives to focus on being productive in the relations with one another rather than focusing on using the government to extort other people. That is so fundamentally important. Well, what happened was, that we ran that experiment for a hundred years.

JUNKIN: And so we are now talking 1870 approximately . . .

B: Yes, and then we had the American Counter-Revolution, also known as the Progressive Era, or the Liberal Progressives in Europe. And that was liberal at that time, in the old Manchester liberal, classic liberal context. So we hit the Counter-Revolution because they didn't understand a lot of things. They had good intentions, I mean they really did. But they didn't understand inventory adjustment. They did not understand capital theory. They didn't understand property rights. And so they looked around America and they said, "Gee, we are really screwing up with natural resources." The problem was one of market failure. They looked at the buffalo, for example. They looked at timber pricing. They looked at pollution. Look, the market doesn't work. A whole variety of things. They were noble goals — I subscribe to their goals; but their analysis was wrong on every count that I've looked at.

For example: their best example is the buffalo, or the passenger pigeon. The problem there was that these were fugitive resources in which there were not private property rights. The only way you got private property rights for the buffalo was to kill it. The only way you could get private property rights to a whale was to kill it. At the same time, the buffalo were almost driven to extinction. We were left with a remnant population in Yellowstone Park. Nobody was worried about Herefords becoming extinct. And Herefords were worth more, I mean on a per animal basis, on a per pound basis. Herefords were worth more than buffalo, and yet people said that because of greed and because the buffalo are worth so much, they are being exterminated. No, sorry; the problem was no private property rights.

Our piece in *Economic Inquiry* on dealing with the Native American as the resource manager . . . did you see that? *Economic Inquiry* the journal of the Western Economics Association. We contrasted the Indians dealing with the beaver and the deal with the buffalo. Now, I know Indians are different, not all Indians are the same — I did time as an anthropologist; I have credentials that are really quite good — but the point is that we had native peoples operating with native institutions and they confronted the beaver and in the early exploitation of the beaver, they did the sensible thing. They established private property rights to the beaver, because they assigned various families or moieties to sections of a stream. That's easy to do. They overharvest one year, they pay the consequences the next. So they ran the beaver as a sustained resource. They were trading with the French by the way. Note that until the French came along, there was no reason to have any regulations at all, because you know, you can only wear so many beaver pelts. Well, in contrast, the Indians, with the buffalo — they couldn't respond that way, because you cannot establish property rights on a buffalo because they are not sedentary. They are fugitive. Okay. So at any rate the progressives didn't understand that. They didn't understand capital theory. They did not understand inventory adjustment. But most important they didn't understand property rights, so they proposed the American Counter-Revolution,

The problem is that the Forest Service is responding exactly as it should respond, given the institution. It reacts to a political calculus. God, in Her infinite wisdom, knows better than to try to grow timber commercially in Utah. The Forest Service doesn't . . .

John Baden

which arrested the process of privatizing these sources. Instead, as a matter of policy, it said, "We are going to have the government manage resources because the private sector can't." And that gave rise to this whole litany and alphabet: BLM, and the antecedents of BLM, Bureau of Reclamation, Forest Service. All of these organizations are populated by individuals who are relatively smart, who are relatively well-intended, and who are relatively well-trained: good people basically, my students. My very best students are in each of these agencies that I just mentioned. Here we had good people, systematically doing horrible things. Really bad things. Why?

Decisions are made on the basis of information and incentives — whether you are saving souls or slaughtering sows. Decisions are made on the basis of information. The only alternative of that was dealing with the same people, some sort of random number generator, which they might occasionally use, but basically now the people make the decisions on the basis of information and incentives. The existing institutional structure systematically generates bad information and incredibly perverse incentives. And this yields outcomes that are economically irrational and environmentally very, very destructive. That's how I approach the public lands.

Let me go on. Let me give you a true, empirical, universal, statistical general assessment. In every society that exists, in every society that has ever existed, and I predict in every society that ever will exist, wealth and political power are positively related. That's point number one.

Point number two: the overwhelming majority of all citizens are rationally ignorant about most issues of public policy — for a very simple reason. Information is expensive in terms of time, even if it is free in terms of money. There are 1200 bills before Congress every year. Now almost nobody except the special interests involved, knows anything about more than two or three of those bills. *Anything!* The average American citizen of voting age cannot name his congressman, let alone know how he voted on each of 1200 votes. So, in every natural resource issue that is both emotional and technically complex — and they all are —

what happens is we always find a coalition of three groups.

That is the iron law of politics. We have the bureaucratic entrepreneurs running the agencies, always wanting to perpetuate, safeguard and expand the agencies' budgets. We have special interests who stand to benefit in one particular case — it could be the ranchers who got more AUM, at what price? This year the price was $1.38. Market price on our ranch we sold for $10.50. One year, we got over $12.00: roughly 10 percent or ten times what we are getting at the federal level. And the third group is the elected politicians. The system rewards behavior. So we have this coalition of three groups: special interest, the bureaucratic entrepreneurs, and the elected officials who bring home the benefits. They concentrate benefits and diffuse the costs.

I spent six months working on the Garrison Diversion Project. Not full time, because I have other things to do. One of the most incredibly stupid projects that has ever been designed. Are you familiar with it?

J: I've taken the dog and pony show tour of it. What is your scenario of the project?

B: Essentially 1.65 million dollars per farm; yeah, 1.65 million dollars per farm. The cost per acre is going to go somewhere between 5,000 and 8,500 per acre. And the land is only worth about 1,100 dollars an acre when they are done with it. Why did that go through? Of course we got to change the bid. Well, it's not an accident that both the North Dakota senators are on the Senate Appropriations Committee. It's just the expected outcome. These are not aberrations. This is the expected outcome. It is perfectly consistent with the logic. Why is it that on the Tongass National Forests — are you familiar with that? — with $92.00 administrative costs per thousand board feet, only $2.00 per thousand board feet was returned to the U.S. Treasury? Where does the lumber go?

J: Japan.

B: That was bad only because it is the most outrageous of all. It is also the biggest forest — 16.4 million acres — in the country. But those outcomes are expected when it is in the public sector. Those simply are expected. If you don't understand the logic of this by now, then I am failing.

J: No, I am understanding. Let's look for a minute at your arguments on timber.

B: I think the Liberal Progressives said, "We marched through [using all the timber in] England in a couple of centuries; that was supposed to last forever. We went through the Great lakes — which was a far larger timber resource — in two and one-half to three decades, and now all we have left is that little corner." And yet, the reality of it is when I was logging in Montana in 1970, there was timber being harvested on contract at $2.00 per thousand board feet — $2.00 per thousand board feet in 1970 — private timber. And that was all it was worth. All that tells us is that the inventory is huge. In an equilibrium, timber should return the same as soy beans, corn, sugar cane, or oranges. Everything should return about the same. If it doesn't, all it means is you have got too much of it. And in terms of commercial viability, we have a huge excess inventory now. You cannot make money growing timber, and make a normal return. Of course part of that reason is because the Feds are there.

J: You mean then, with the feds putting too much — or too little on the market?

B: No. Look, it's simple. It is simpler than that. Don't make the problem hard, because it is really easy. The problem is that the Forest Service is responding exactly as it should respond, given the institution. It reacts to a political calculus. God, in Her infinite wisdom, know-better than to try to grow timber commercially in Utah. The Forest Service doesn't. That's my quote. The point is very simple.

I mean (Utah Senators) Hatch and Garn — great conservatives, right? Now do you think they walk into Appropriations and say, "Do you know that at the Forest Service, you are spending X million dollars a year growing commercial timber in Utah, and that is really silly, so please don't spend anymore in Utah?" Well, of course not. They would go in and say, "You know, we need a bigger timber budget for Utah." Why? Because of those poor Mormon towns. You are talking GS salaries. A GS 9 in southern Utah is making big money. GS 14 for a supervisor. Wow! I mean that's like a doctor. And that's a big deal for a local community, and the fact that it doesn't make any sense in the total picture is irrelevant. So the problem is that decisions are made politically. See, we are cutting too little timber some places and far too much in others. They were cutting too much timber in the San Juans in Colorado. In most of the forests in Oregon and Washington, they are not cutting nearly enough. Let me tell you of an example — this is a true story. There was a forest in Northern California. It had a cut of X — I don't know what X was, but it had a cut of X. A forest fire destroyed about 20 percent of the unit, so they had to re-establish the cut, right? The cut went up to 2X. Why? Doesn't that sound crazy? It's true; given their formula, that is the only way it could come out. They have a non-declining even flow constraint on timber — non-declining yield, even flow. You got all this timber sitting here that is 600 years of age and it is going downhill slowly — that is it is dying and rotting faster than it is growing. You can only cut X million board feet per year and that's based on what is being produced in this forest. If you wipe out 20 percent of that old stuff, instantaneously, it is growing new stuff; so you have dramatically increased the amount of growth through a forest fire — because the X thousand acres that used to be "decadent" are now thriving. So that means that you can double your cut or however the numbers came out, which happened to be double on what was remaining.

J: Yes, but this growth is still going to take another 90-100 years to be even close to a forest rather than a stand of young trees.

A ll I'm prepared to do is say, "Look, under my system I assume the people are self-interested and will design it so that self-interested people will behave in socially responsible ways. Design a system, such that the information and signs produced are such that self-interested people will behave in socially responsible and beneficial ways. And if they want to do additional good on top of that, because they happened to be nice people . . . that's fine. That's wonderful. That ought to even make it easier . . . but let's not rely upon it." That's all I am saying.

There is clearly some value in having the resources there, but that value for the future will be maximized if the management is in private hands. The relevant discount rate in the public sector approaches infinity, beyond, two, four or six years, because everything is in terms of the next election . . . The public lands are best understood as things that are being exchanged to advance special interest, elected officials and bureaucrats. This isn't going to make me very popular.

John Baden

B: No, no no. In that country it probably should be looking at 50 years, roughly, I don't know. Relatively short, but the point is that it is there, and it is growing and within that logic, which would have made perfect sense. But all that tells you is to liquidate that old growth. But I say — and this is what I have always advocated — look, there are some ecological communities dependent upon old growth, and they have a value.

We can't sell that in the market, not directly. We have nature conservationists and organizations like that who provide some of it, but not enough in my judgment. And so let's set this aside carefully. Just set them aside and let them go. And then cut that other stuff. Get rid of it.

But what I'd rather do is get rid of the Forest Service. It is so bad, it's predictably bad. It is not bad people. That is so important. Standard environmentalists' analysis of the problem — it's so sophisticated: "Gee, there are bad people in there. Solution: let's replace them with good people." It's nuts. Or a slightly worse version of it is, "Gee, people are self-interested. Let's replace self-interest with altruism toward other people than God's creatures." I don't know what to say other than I'll pray for you. What else can you say? It is ridiculous.

J: You suddenly jump back 450 years and argue whether man is inherently evil?

B: No. All I'm prepared to do is say, "Look, under my system I assume the people are self-interested and will design it so that self-interested people will behave in socially responsible ways. Design a system, such that the information and signs produced are such that self-interested people will behave in socially responsible and beneficial ways. And if they want to do additional good on top of that, because they happened to be nice people . . . that's fine. That's wonderful. That ought to even make it easier . . . but let's not rely upon it." That's all I am saying.

J: Okay. Let's take a brief look at your national parks' proposal.

B: I think we should be dealing with parks and wilderness areas as independent public corporations similarly to whatever corporation there is for the Metropolitan Museum [in New York] for example. It is not a governmental agency. And they should have title to the thing — to the park, to the wilderness, to whatever.

Now, we don't want to start with Yellowstone Park, obviously, because you are talking about an experiment and you don't start with something that serious, but you start with something that is really not that visible and something that is not that important, and you transfer membership, ownership, to this public, non-profit corporation that is set up with a mission in the same way that the Metropolitan Museum Board has trustees subject to the common law document of trust — well-developed over the past six centuries, at least. They have this mission of fostering whatever it is — preservation of park values, or wildlife or whatever — and they control the resource. If they want to buy advertising time, they can do that. If they want to sell some Picassos to get some Rembrandts, they can do that. If they want to lease out their place for a reception, they can do that.

Now take the Targhee National Forest, which is in this critical Yellowstone ecosystem. We have this area down here in Palisades where we know there is oil and gas. No question. The question is how much and the question is where. Well, right now, the environmental groups have absolutely zero reason to encourage or indeed even tolerate development of oil or gas from the Palisades, which is a long way from the park, by the way — it is just the south end of the forest.

Look, what would happen if we had a Targhee Endowment group to manage this forest for multiple use. I would actually prefer that all the members focus on the conservation and ecological and maybe historical, in some cases, values of the forest rather than the timber, for instance.

What would they do if someone told them there is oil and gas there? They'd say, "Great. Wonderful. The question is how can we get it out with the least damage, with the greatest potential for reversibility — which is very easy by, the way — and how can we maximize our return? Because with all this habitat we want to buy, the limiting factor in the Targhee is winter range."

J: So you're saying that it would become in the best interest of the board to keep the park, as a park — viable, beautiful — and that the goal would have my total interest, as a board member, not because it happened to be in my state or because I have politically balance the special interest groups.

B: Notice how all the calculations change? Right now if you were a Forest Service superintendent, and someone tells you that you have oil and gas in there, you would say, "Oh no. Not me. Anything but oil and gas." And you'd get nothing for it. Nothing. Even now if you asked the guy, you said, "Gee, could you use another couple hundred thousand a year in your budget?" I mean he'd sell his grandmother for that, because they do care about their forest. They genuinely care about their forests and there are all these things that they would love to do, and all they can get money for is to build roads. They can always get money to build roads. And I talk about this to environmentalists and they think I'm nuts.

J: Why?

B: Criticizing public ownership on efficiency grounds is analogous to criticizing Holy Communion on nutritional grounds to these people. They are sylvan socialists, you know. I don't know how else — I have given up on other explanations. Some are smart enough that you can, you know, have enough intellectual integrity that you can walk them through and they then say, "Gee, I never thought about the problem that way or the issue that way before. Clearly this makes sense. Yeah, I'll have to reevaluate what I am doing."

J: Let me give you these questions, now that we have some of your arguments down.

B: Do you really want me to do those questions?

J: The first question is how do you perceive the value of the public lands?

B: I can't answer questions like that.

J: Okay. But let me tell you what I was trying to get at. The point is if we have a population of Easterners who have never seen the public lands in the West, what do you say when they say, "Look, I understand that almost 50 percent of the west is federally managed, so what good do I get from them? What good are they doing me if I live in Massachusetts? How would you describe the value of the public lands. What are we going to use them for? Should we allow them to be privatized — is there no value if they are in public hands?

B: Public lands are used as mediums of exchange among politicians to evoke special interests. That is how they are being used. Now the public gets some benefit from it and the public can, in fact, the wealthy public can, visit Yellowstone Park, Glacier Park and all the national forests at essentially zero admission cost. But basically your public lands are horribly mismanaged in terms of efficiency and in terms of environment.

J: Do the resources for the future exist in the public lands? Is that what we should be looking to them for? Is that one of their inherent values — that the resources have been set aside — out of private use?

B: There is clearly some value in having the resources there, but that value for the future will be maximized if the management is in private hands. The relevant discount rate in the public sector approaches infinity, beyond, two, four or six years, because everything is in terms of the next election. Look at minerals, or energy on the public lands. It is all, every contract, due dilligence

contract. If you believe, for example, that a mineral is more valuable, or oil and gas would be more valuable in the future, you
cannot leave it to the future. You have to exercise due-dilligence
in getting it out of the ground now, or you lose your lease. It is
very simple: the calculations are off. The public lands are best
understood as things that are being exchanged to advance special
interest, elected officials and bureaucrats. This isn't going to
make me very popular.

J: Do you think you are popular now?

B: I have some very positive constructive things to say and that
is not what this is doing. That's why I hooked the early part.

J: I'm just trying to figure out a phrase for what the best use of
the public lands might be from your perspective.

B: I can't answer that.

J: I understand that . . .

B: Look, different public lands are best used for different things.
Most of the commercial forest classified as such is not commercial forest at all. I mean, timber likes to grow where it is
warm, wet and low. Most of the public lands are high, dry and
cold. And the Forest Service happens to classify it as commercial
forest. That does not mean it is commercial forest. I could classify our ranches as banana plantations and people would laugh at
me. But the Forest Service can classify stuff with very little rain,
very high elevation, very dry, as commercial forest, and people
say, "Oh, it must be commercial forest." That's nuts. So, there is
some commercial forest land — and that should be transferred to
the private sector by a simple auction — and if you don't put this
down, I ill be very annoyed — with covenants and with ease-
ments to protect ecological and recreational resources.

J: Let's get to the last two questions. Let's look a hundred years into the future. What would you like to see? Describe your vision for the public lands. Is it different from today?

B: What I would like to see with the public lands, one hundred years in the future, looking back. Let's move to the Tricentennial of the U.S. Constitution, 2087. Let's look back from 2087 to now and we would find there was the American Revolution and the associated constitution. Then there was the Counter-Revoluion associated with the Progressive Era. There was then the Counter-Counter-Revolution that gained national significance in 1987.

Then the following century was the century in which the original ideas of the founders were again implemented and the vast majority of the public lands were transferred to either non-profit conservation groups in the private sector, or to commercial, profit-seeking corporations. The federal government ended up holding a few things, like Yellowstone Park. That was on a management-contract basis, by the way, by private outfits, because you get these incredible things when the Park Service is maintaining its own vehicles. The cost is probably three times what it could be done for by private contractors. And yet the political pressure of trying to get it changed in the vehicles is so bad, you can't even get that done, which is nuts.

J: From our position in 2087, how would we assess the land policies today? What would we say about them as historians, looking back?

B: We would say, "Look. From the Progressive Era — from the centennial of the Constitution until the bicentennial of the Constitution — we relied on a myth of scientific management as probably best articulated by Pinchot. That century was essentially a century of gathering data on the realities of "scientific management." The data came in over a hundred years, and the data consistently showed that decisions made were not the decisions that detached scientific expert managers could, in some sense, divine. They could not predict the demand schedules and preference functions of the citizens, who at that time are a hundred years in the future."

But rather, the citizens were in accord with the political calculus. And that data came in and people said, "Hey, you know, the founders had a better idea in 1787." And they went back to that. But it is too bad it took a hundred years of study to do that.

June, 1985
Denver, Colorado

ROD NASH

Roderick Nash is a professor of History and Environmental Studies at the University of California at Santa Barbara. He first raised eyebrows when he suggested that use of the wilderness is a privilege and not a right. Concurrently, he advocates that people who use the wilderness be trained and licensed, much as hunters are, before they are allowed to use the nation's wilderness as recreation areas. His book, Wilderness and the American Mind, *marks an era in which thought about wilderness has come of age. As he notes, wilderness is no longer considered a threat, but is instead a necessity.*

NASH: As a historian, I have great enthusiasm for the concept of keeping certain key environmental resources in public as opposed to individual hands. I think that one of the great ideas of the American frontier process was that in this age of rampant individualism and privatization, we were able to identify and set aside public property with the concept that nobody can own the land, and then do with it what they want. What I compare it to when I teach my students is slavery. We had the idea of owning an individual, and we abolished slavery. There are some of the same constraints working in terms of land, it seems to me. The fact that you are married to someone, doesn't give you the right to beat that person. The fact that you hire someone to work for

It seems to me we are sending two-year-olds into the wilderness today. And in many cases they are destroying the resource. They have certainly destroyed the experience for other people and they may be endangering themselves and search and rescue people. The wilderness is so fragile, so rare now, and demand for it so great, that I think a time has come to begin to think about licensing them, like the licensed drivers on the roads or pilots in the sky or scuba divers under the water.

Rod Nash

you is a business relationship, not a slave relationship. But the land is the last of a series of entities, if you will, to be liberated. The beginning of the liberation was the identification that no one person can acquire, buy, take land and then do with it what they want, anymore than you can abuse a child that may be yours or your wife's or beat your husband, whatever.

So I go back to 1641, the Great Ponds Act, as the root of all of this. In Massachusetts, today, for any pond over 10 acres in size, you have to provide public access and allow the public to come and fish on it. If you and I were fortunate enough to own a piece of land on which there was a ten-acre lake, or over ten acres, we could not put up a great big sign that said "KEEP OFF."

Now that idea has been extended and is still on the books in Massachusetts, so that the recognition was that there was an environmental resource here that had a transcendent value and that one individual could not own it. Of course that extended into the national park idea, which Wallace Stegner said was the best idea this country ever had, to the national forest concept, to the BLM concept, to all of these, as well as to our management of rivers. And we have to look at things like the Federal Water Power Act of 1920, which told Henry Ford, who wanted at that time to buy a site on the Tennessee River called Muscle Shoals he would not be able to do that. We don't want one private individual, no matter how rich he is, acquiring something as vital in the environmental scheme of things as a major river. That, I think, was a very good insight, and of course led on to the TVA [Tennessee Valley Authority]. Because without Ford there, then Roosevelt was able to come in and put TVA through.

The same with the coast line out here in California where we have identified the need for coastal access and no matter whether you are Jane Fonda or whoever, you cannot buy the beach. You can buy a house on the beach, but you can't prevent the public from walking down the beach, and there has to be certain accesses through the property at Malibu and other coast lines to get to the beach.

This is all a concept of public lands. It is, to me, very, very exciting. What it represents is a sort of midway station between capitalism and socialism. Now we don't like the word socialism in this country and we have always avoided it. We use words like nationalism, but what we really have in the public lands is a form of socialism, a form of collective ownership, a form of common ownership. I'm sure there would be great champions of the National Forests and the BLM lands who would scream in horror if someone told them, "Well you know what you are really dealing with is a communistic arrangement of ownership." But that in fact is what we are dealing with. And I think it represents, as I say, the best part of the communistic/socialistic ideas. Sort of a way station, just as we know the Russians have altered their communism to accept a good deal of individual initiative — capitalistic behavior.

JUNKIN: And so along with that concept of communal ownership, is that what the value would be to someone who won't necessarily ever walk through the public lands, that you and I can enjoy on any given day?

N: That's right. People who believe in tempering rampant capitalism with some sort of social purpose would applaud this. And this is the whole idea of the public lands. So that is my thinking about the value and the concept, I see it going back historically and I see it representing a sort of alternative to the main thrust of American history, which was get the land, put a fence up around it, it's yours, do with it what you want. And that I like.

Now a very important step in all of this was the Taylor Grazing Act of 1934, which, in effect, ended the frontier. Now we say the frontier ended in 1890, because that was when the census was requested. But for my purposes, the real frontier ended in 1934 when we simply said we are not going to continue to hand out land anymore to people. We are going to retain all the land that has not been claimed in public ownership. That, in effect, created the Bureau of Land Management, which was originally called the General Land Office. And that was the end of an era.

You know — an end of the real era. For 200 years we had directed all of our energies toward giving, alienating the public
domain, that concept: getting it into private hands, as fast as possible. And now finally we came to the end of that road, and we
decided that we would hold onto what was left. Of course the
Dust Bowl and some of the events of the thirties that seemed to
the people to be linked to unwise private practices on land, figured into that.

J: One thing I have been noting both in the history of the Forest
Service and BLM is the notion between right and privilege, with
regard to use and/or access to the public lands. Do you see that
as a keystone issue on wilderness as well?

N: I have argued very strongly that access to wilderness should
not be regarded as a right, but rather a privilege to be earned, and
that in fact, I went so far in *Backpacker* and in a couple of other
magazines and I think even in *Newsweek* — that article your office did — to talk about a Wilderness License. The idea that the
only people who are allowed to go into wilderness have demon-
strated that they are responsible to be given that privilege — just
like crossing the street. When you are old enough to cross the
street, your mother lets you, but you didn't send two-year-olds
out there. It seems to me we are sending two-year-olds into the
wilderness today. And in many cases they are destroying the
resource. They have certainly destroyed the experience for other
people and they may be endangering themselves and also search
and rescue people. And wilderness is so fragile, so rare now,
and demand for it so great, that I think a time has come to begin
to think about licensing them [wilderness users], like the licensed
drivers on the roads or pilots in the sky or scuba divers under the
water.

In fact, the idea of right and privilege is the very heart of
this American sense of "the land is mine, I can do with it what I
want to." That has been tempered by the idea that the land is
different from owning your car, buddy. You can go to your car,
you can spill oil on it, you can dump beer in it, you can smash it

*I*n fact, the idea of right and privilege is the very heart of this American sense of "the land is mine, I can do with it what I want to." That has been tempered by the idea that the land is different from owning your car, buddy. You can go to your car, you can spill oil on it, you can dump beer in it, you can smash it up, you can neglect it, but that's "your" car, right? But you don't own the land, and if you do that, it is to the detriment of other forms of life and future generations and other people as well. So society steps in and says you can't do that.

Rod Nash

up, you can neglect it, but that's "your" car, right? But you don't own the land, and if you do that, it is to the detriment of other forms of life and future generations and other people as well. So society steps in and says you can't do that.

One of the great values of this land, it seems to me, and one that ought to be right up there with grazing and watershed and mining, is space and solitude. Whether you call it wilderness or whether you call it applesauce, it doesn't make any difference to me. The wilderness has become kind of a bug-a-boo word. You know, a fighting word. And it seems to me what's really important is to keep the spaciousness and the openness, and to keep the MX missiles out, to keep the high-tech out, windmills and solar power — I include that. And if you have a little grazing, fine. You have a couple of dirt roads and take a truck over them once in a while, fine. But the "wilderness" sometimes gets a little too pure. And in doing that they have excluded from their consideration a lot of land with extraordinary wilderness on it. I am even applying more to this conversation right now, more wildness than the "wilderness." Do you see what I'm saying?

J: Yes, I do understand, but I see the problem of trying to describe not just alpine wilderness but BLM wilderness to somebody who lives in New York City. And their response to the BLM lands is, "Where are mountain peaks?" and "You know, this is not pretty, this is not beautiful, this is not inspiring, except maybe of fear more than inspiring beauty."

N: That's why we have learned so much in recent years from people like Ann Winger, and Edward Abbey and others who have told us that there is value in places that were long overlooked. That's what we began to learn from the Santa Fe writers and artists like Georgia O'Keefe and the others. You are right — the conventional aesthetics don't identify with any value of Mexican Hat at all. All they see is a bunch of rocks out there.

I talked to a guy at Glen Canyon Dam — I was coming back across Glen Canyon with the students on this trip and we were discussing the pros and cons of the dam — and I said,

"You know, sir, this dam has a shoreline of 1800 miles and it goes back 186 miles up there, so it is not just this dam you are talking about. You are talking about Lake Powell. And he was a guy — snowhaired from Ohio or someplace — and he looked out over the country and said, "Well, that's just wasteland out there." He says, "This is the best use for it, isn't it?"

And I said, "Yeah." I was trying to be nice with him. I said, "Well, you know that there are some people who think that the land had a good deal of value in its natural condition, as Glen Canyon." And the kids were all chuckling, you know, because this guy didn't know who he was talking to or what was going on, but he was just a classic caricature, well-meaning, but "Gosh, it doesn't look like Ohio, Martha . . ." and "You know, it's just more and more rocks out there and more and more sun and more and more rattlesnakes and tarantulas" and that's the view of the desert.

J: Let's move on to what you think the best use is of the public lands — and I am looking at all the agency lands as a whole. We can talk multiple use or not, but what I'm wondering is, as a society or as individuals, what should we look to the public lands for in the future?

N: Well, I think first and foremost, we should look to the public lands as providing a base of environmental integrity. That it is an ongoing enduring environmental resource where wild things can live, where spiritual values can be generated, in other words, I am talking about nonconsumptive uses. I think they represent a kind of anchor to windward. A storm anchor for our society that is rushing headlong and pall mall into an uncertain future. And I think the greatest value of these lands is not going to be in terms of utilitarian values — in terms of lumber or the grasses, or the beef that might be carved out of them, but rather it is going to be as — and I am not using the term wilderness here — an environmental backlog for a civilization that is changing other parts of the environment so rapidly and so radically. And that's what I see as one of the primary values in the next hundred years. If we

have a hundred years. That's going to be a fairly radical idea,
you see, because I'm not talking in utilitarian terms at all here.

J: Let's look 100 years into the future — and I know you have
already partially answered this question — but what is a view
that you would like to have of the public lands? I mean, what is
your vision of it from your house, or from Mexican Hat? What is
it that you would like to see?

N: Right. Well, I look out over maybe 200,000 square miles
from my ranch in Moab, Utah, onto public lands. I'd like to see
them in 100 years remain essentially as they are, or possibly
even show some improvement in terms of range, which will
necessitate some restraint on the part of the users.

It may be that we have asked too much of it. Maybe we ask
too much of Yellowstone when we permit 2 million visitors a
year in there. Maybe we ask too much of the Grand Canyon
when we float 16,000 people a year down that river. Maybe we
ask too much in terms of animal month units, or whatever the
hell it is called; maybe we overstress the grasses.

I would like to see a little more restraint. And I would like
to see that restraint also extend to wilderness users who have to
realize that wilderness, like tennis, is a game played with few
people and you can't have everybody in there. And that is going
to require waiting turns, like you do for a tennis court, signing
up at odd seasons, and in other ways, monitoring your use of the
public lands.

And I would hope that a hundred years in the future, we do
not look at the public lands, as I fear we are doing now, as the
guy said, "wasteland." Places where we can do anything else we
want, like put in MX missiles, like dump radioactive waste, all
of which are happening in my front yard over there. Like bring
in wind farms and solar power towers, and here you know I
depart from the conventional rhetoric that says those are good
things because they are soft tech. I am saying that I think they are
very good and certainly better than Glen Canyon Dam, and nu-

clear power plants. But to just look at a piece of vacant land —
and here I am speaking particularly of the BLM lands — and
say, "Well, there is nothing there, so why don't we put up 500
wind machines." Now we are not talking about dutch girls with
tulips. We are talking about big stuff, and this worries me a great
deal, because I feel a lot of well-meaning people and some of my
colleagues will get rapidly into the wind energy area. And using
the best sites, which always tend to be the highest sites — you
can't have underground wind power — and they bring an element of the 22nd century into essentially a 17th century setting. I
am concerned about the logic that says, "Oh well, they are public
lands and you are only taking 10 square feet for a windmill, so if
nothing else is going on out there, go ahead and do it."

From my standpoint, if you and I are standing looking out
over a series or ridges and we see a 200-foot wind machine or
500 of them, or a power tower, like the one they have on the Mo-
jave Desert that you can see for 150 miles, you have totally
changed the aesthetics of the area. I am asking for restraint in regard to that. The basic point is not to regard the public lands as
vacant, but regard them as full of values. And those values are
only to be superseded or moved aside, after careful consideration
of other values, and that represents a certain change in American
thinking.

J: If we were historians looking back one hundred years from
our position in the future, how would we assess our generation
today?

N: Well, I think we'd look back on this generation as one that
was really making the final decisions with regard to the American
frontier. I tell my students the Taylor Grazing Act of 1934 was
the end. But I also tell them that today is the real end of the American Frontier, because we are making final, and to the most extent, irreversible decisions in terms of the national forests. We
have had the RARE inventories, we have decided what areas are
to be used, and what areas to be put in wilderness and what areas
to be studied. BLM is going through that process and by the end

The basic point is not to regard the public lands as vacant, but to regard them as full of values, now. And those values are only to be superseded or moved aside, after careful consideration of other values, and that represents a certain change in American thinking.

Rod Nash

of the century will have completed it. National parks have largely
been created. I don't think another big national park will be created in the lower 48 states. Alaska was divided in 1980 and apportioned out. We don't have another Alaska treading along in space
that we are going to be able to use. So in point of fact, this is the
generation, right now.

It's frightening to look at those maps of the public lands:
they are full of colors, right? Colors for this kind of use and that
kind of use and motorized recreation and you realize this is like
dividing up the raiment of Jesus, or something. I'm not very religious; I forget what that metaphor was, but there was something there. This is really cutting things up and apportioning it
out. And this is what our generation is doing. And we have been
putting the land into categories.

So the decisions we make I hope are good ones, and I hope
the future generations on looking back a hundred years, will look
at us and say, "Hey, those people in the 1980s and 1990s, they
made some good decisions because they created the legacy — the
environmental legacy — that we inherited."

I hope they won't look back and say, "Those #$% in effect
stole from us the right or the privilege of experiencing the big
horn sheep, or solitude," or whatever it was and I think that we
really have to answer to the future in that way. I sometimes compare it to the intellectuals of Nazi Germany, who in later years,
were asked, "Where were you guys when Adolph Hitler rose
up? Why didn't you say anything?" Why were you just — and I
am thinking now of people like myself — writers, professors,
why were you just in the universities in your ivory towers? Why
didn't you say something? Why didn't you do something? Why
did you just let this thing happen?

And I say almost the same thing now in regard to Mr. Reagan and Mr. Watt. You know that the people concerned, the
writers, the intellectuals, the professors, the teachers have a responsibility, lest someone 100 years from now points the finger
back at them and say, "You know, where the hell were you? You
know, Nash and all you people, and Bernie Shanks — why
didn't you people do more? Why did you let the Grand Canyon

be dammed?" David Brower didn't let it be dammed; that was one of the great achievements. That's what I'm concerned about.

If we can direct our action today, day by day, with the thought that 100 years from now, when open space is even more important than today, how will someone look back on the decisions that we made now, which are really the final decisions, you see. We don't have another National Park System, or National Forest System, to work on if we blow it with this one. You know, this is it. And so that's the excitement but also sort of the sobering responsibility.

J: I have read many of your books about the change in attitude that have people suddenly looking at the Frontier as no longer something to conquer, but something to actually protect. What was it? What was it that turned the tide on that?

N: Well, I think it was the ending of the Frontier, the running out of the Frontier. You see for a long time — and this is a basic thesis of *Wilderness and the American Mind* — for a long time nature was bigger than the population in this country. And initially it was dominant. I mean wilderness was everything west of Plymouth Rock. Then gradually, as we extended our control over the environment, there was more parity between the two. And then gradually toward the end of the 19th century, civilization prevailed. And eventually we have reduced wilderness to where about two percent of the lower 48 states is probably going to end up as designated. You know what I mean by that wilderness status — two percent when it was 100 percent. And I think it is that swing, that change in the environmental conditions, the fact that more people grew up staring at walls than they did staring at forest walls, that produced the change in attitude. Where wilderness became a novelty, right? Where it became somthing different, something exciting, something refreshing, something to look back on with nostalgia, something to regard as an heirloom or a historical document, or an era that once contained a lot of glory and excitement — the Frontier Era. And I think — and I'm talking now about the average person, not the scholar, or the kind that read Thoreau and Emerson's books — but for the average person, it was a shift in environmental conditions. The perception that the country was becoming middle-aged, that it had lost its youth, and that somehow, wilderness was bound up with its youth and bound up with those great days of growth and those great excitements, that one sector called geography and hope. And I think as more and more people lived in Denver, you know, they could begin to look at the wilderness a great deal differently than people who had crossed on covered wagons and lived in pioneer cabins. So it was that change in environmental circumstance, which you can see paralleled in Europe and everywhere else. Jean Jacques Rousseau was not exactly your basic pioneer, right? He could talk about the Noble Savage because he didn't have any in his culture.

J: Is it not too romantic though to attribute so much of the American spirit, if you will, to the wilderness and to the Frontier?

N: Well, I think wilderness was the basic raw material from which this civilization was shaped. If there is anything that sets us apart from other parts of the world, it was that in the last 200 years, we dealt with a substantial encounter — we created substantial encounter between civilization and wilderness. And I don't know whether that is romantic or not. I think it is just being historical. Many of the characteristics and traits of our culture — and I'm going, of course, back to Frederick Jackson Turner's ideas — I believe, stem from this experience. You can call it a Frontier. You can call it Wilderness. Or you can simply call it Opportunity in Abundance that we're faced with here. Producing respect for the individual, producing a practicality, producing some of our best and worst characteristics.

Santa Barbara, California
May 1985

JAMES B. THOMPSON _____

Jim Thompson, Superintendent of Rocky Mountain National Park, is a career park service ranger. He started his service in Rocky Mountain National Park in the early sixties. Perhaps he was one of the rangers who first taught me that classic national park ethic: "Don't pick the wildflowers (or any other resource, including rocks and antlers); What if everyone did? Then there would be no wildflowers for any one else to enjoy. Let's leave them so that everyone can enjoy them." That person in a uniform bending down to a young child instills a powerful memory and a powerful ethic that some things are best, when they are simply left alone to be enjoyed. Thompson has done a tour through the national parks, serving at Rocky Mountain for the last several years.

JUNKIN: Let me start first by launching into the habitat-versus-people argument. It's one of the conflicts a national park always faces. Is there any way to decide who comes first, or what the primary use of the national park must be?

THOMPSON: Well, not really. You know, this park was established in 1915, about a year and one-half prior to the establishment of the National Park Service. So it is the National Park Service Act which says conserve scenery, and throws up conservation and use — or visitor enjoyment — as two components of the formula. That [clarification of purpose of the National Parks] came a year and one-half after the establishment of the park. But the (act that set aside the) park here had very similar language, yet in some ways more precise. I always keep it here in my desk . . . now I probably won't be able to find it . . . let me just read it to you:

"Dedicated and set apart as a public park for the benefit and enjoyment of the people of the United States with regulations being primarily aimed at the freest use of the said park for recreational purposes by the public and for preservation of the natural conditions and scenic beauties thereof."

Well, it is very similar language to the National Park Service Act but it very precisely uses the words "recreational use and preservation of the natural conditions." It doesn't say, "or". It doesn't say one or the other; it says both. And so we have to figure that since they said about the same thing twice, that they really meant it. And of those who call for more development, or those who call for less recreational opportunities or less development of the park, both would prefer to emphasize one of those things over the other. What we have to do is not necessarily compromise. What we have to do is do both, and that just can't be reduced to a simple kind of a statement, which, to me, is a gross oversimplification of the problem. It is the challenge, or whatever you want to call it. And people who sit on one side of the fence or the other usually oversimplify and say, "Well, this is what was intended. This is what it says." And frankly, I don't find that it is very useful to argue with them.

J: Is it possible to do both, do you think?

T: There is no question that we can do both, to some degree. And it is always a matter of degree. In almost everything you do — in almost every kind of decision that you make. Even preservation — absolute preservation — means very, very different things to different people. You have, for example, those who would say that preservation means letting things completely alone, hands off. And at the same time, those people will say we should reintroduce the wolf. If we reintroduce the wolf, that's not a hands-off sort of thing; that's manipulative. And I'm not saying that manipulative is bad. There are those who feel manipulative is preservation. So there are always degrees of these things that can be so easily oversimplified, and that's a very convenient thing to do if you are in this job. So doing both is always a matter of predicting results from different scenarios, measuring the results of those scenarios, and then trying to make the adjustments that are necessary.

When it says something like allowing the freest use for recreational purposes — it doesn't say consistent with, it just

says: "and preservation of the natural resources." So what we try
to do is to identify how recreational use will affect natural conditions, and if we don't feel that recreational use will allow the
preservation of the natural conditions, then we try to channel or
direct it, restructure it in some way. That's really the basics of
park management.

J: I've often wondered whether, from your side of the desk: do
you have a sense that people come here to see a museum, or a
gallery, or that sort of thing, or a park — a piece of the nation's
west, a piece of the natural resources?

T: I think the public comes here to see a park, as well as those
constitutents who maybe visit a park, but still have an interest in
coming with as broad a sense of expectation, as would the public
on any issue. Too many people who are not really familiar with
national parks, interpret the word, the generic word "park" so
broadly that it may reflect something out of their own experience:
a city park down the street which has the bench, shelter and fountains, and maybe a statue. And they really don't know what to
expect. There are people who are dedicated park-goers. There are
wilderness trippers, if you want to call them that, whose interest
is in hiking, backpacking, wild lands, and you bring all of those
different kinds of people together. The fact remains that the
people who have come to this particular park represent all the
states, quite a few foreign countries, and yet, the largest portion
of them are from certain specific geographic areas, and they
bring with them their regional attitudes and interests. So if you
are looking in a statistical sense, you can somewhat predict what
people are looking for, and there are about half of them that come
to this park, that come out of state and most of those come from
the midwest. The other half comes from within Colorado, which
is a growing trend.

J: What is the place of the park system in the public lands in the
western United States? What is their role?

*Y*ou know, the majority of
people tend to think of accomplishment in terms of change.
And we are in such a rapidly changing society that people
need to have something that they can say, "This has not
changed. This remains always the same." I think it is a basic
craving and I think that's a role that the parks can fulfill. It
doesn't really have to be the wild natural parks, but preserving some of the old cultural features of the country. Whether
it is Mesa Verde or Grant's Tomb, I suppose.

I think there is a need to be able to go back to places and
find them unchanged. That's something you can't do about
your home. There are very few of us any more, particularly
urban people, who are born and raised and carry out their
careers and die in the same town. We all move around and
when we go back to the old home, well, it's different. The
house is gone. It's been replaced by a shopping mall. There
are some real needs in us all to be able to go back and find
something that we can remember, that we can pass on to our
children. "This is what my father showed me." And I really
think the only opportunities are in public ownership.

James B. Thompson

T: As you look around the room, there are all kinds of categories of protected lands, and our national parks are the most protected of those that really allow visitors to come into them. The national parks in England, for example, are basically just rural areas with boundaries drawn around them where they try to do some zoning. They may include little protected reserves within them, but they are farmland that is just basically kept in the rural setting, and recreational use is allowed among those kinds of things.

This is very much a concept throughout the rest of the world, where there are not federally-owned lands that are set aside for national parks. So I think that we have something that is really unique, even though there are national parks in many other countries in the rest of the world. But we have probably the most extensive system of fully protected areas, where natural processes and natural conditions are preserved as best we can and people are still allowed to use the areas. And I feel that is a very, very important concept: that we have different categories of public lands for public use.

It is frightening to think I am going to visit England, Scotland and Wales this summer, and I would like to go fishing because I am a big fly fisherman, and there are very few, if any, places that I can just go on publicly-owned lands and fish; it is all privately owned. You have to get permission from the owners, which is very much true throughout Europe. We preserved some concepts of public ownership in this country that allow the general public to use some of these recreational opportunities.

I think it is a preservation of the American spirit really, because it is what this country has always been all about: it preserves that bit of frontier experience that really was part of the development of this country and its purposes, its ideals. You know, we fled from those very conditions. As a people, whether we were Germans or Poles or English or Scottish or whatever, we fled from those kinds of conditions to develop a different system, and to me this is preserving part of that spirit.

J: What is going to be the purpose of these lands 10, 25, 50, 100 years hence? What role will they serve to us?

T: The more scarce anything becomes, the more valuable it becomes. And scarcity can be measured not only in terms of supply, but also in terms of demand. The supply is certainly not going to grow. The demand is going to increase, and therefore, the value is going to increase. It's going to be more important as the population grows, as the development of undeveloped land in private ownership increases. The demands are going to be even greater on the public lands in every sense, not only from the consumptive standpoint but from the non-consumptive standpoint as well. There will be fewer opportunities for recreation, I think, on private land, even though many of those may be devoted to recreation opportunities. Thus, on publicly-owned lands, whether they be state parks, city parks, or recreation areas of various sorts, there will be those increasing demands. And I think that the values will increase. Therefore, we should be all the more concerned about what direction they take, about protecting and preserving those options.

There has been a lot of discussion about more logical management units. I know the Forest Service and BLM are talking about some exchanges. Then there are efforts to reduce some of the outlying units that are hard to manage. That's not what I'm talking about.

What I'm talking about are the broader principles of those lands that are available for recreational use as well as commodities, because so many of them have the concept of multiple use that the Forest Service and BLM pursue. This is a rare thing throughout the world. The fact is other countries don't have single-use areas like national parks, or they have just a few of them. That doesn't mean that they don't have multiple use either. You have single uses of other types, where the land is completely taken over, such as many African countries, where grazing is the use of the land to the exclusion of the erosion control, crop land and a lot of other kinds of opportunities. I think that the multiple use concept is a very interesting land-use concept that really is only beginning to catch on in other parts of the world.

J: Do you think that we can look at parks as being the top of the layer for preservation? I guess I'm also asking whether we could also be looking at it in its role as habitat and as a genetic pool?

T: Well, certainly any protected area has that potential, and it has long been argued that that concept of a genetic pool is possibly one of the most important roles of a park to play. We have re-searched natural areas designated in Rocky Mountain National Park where we don't permit certain types of use. We don't per-mit overnight use, for example, except by researchers. Day use is permitted, but not overnight use. And that's basically the concept there.

I recall attending a hearing in Olympic National Park about ten years ago and the whole discussion was in regard to wasted timber — that wasn't available for cutting — and among all of the foresters, timber cutters, and loggers, one individual got up. He was the biggest, toughest, meanest-looking individual in the whole room and he obviously had just gotten off of work. He got up and it turns out that he must have been a highly educated forester. I don't know who he worked for or if it was his own business, or whatever, but he got into pretty technical detail on modern practices in forestry, fertilization, and he ended up say-ing, "But we in Olympic National Park have the biggest trees, bigger than anything anywhere. We have cut down all the rest of the big trees and we planted inferior stock, which is fertilized. It grows faster and does all those things, but what happens some-day when we get to the point that we can't use those methods anymore? We are going to have to go back and find out why these huge old trees in Olympic have gotten so big, have sur-vived fire, have survived storms. Why? Why are they better than the other trees? Those are the future." And I was dumbfounded.

The majority of the people there didn't even know what he was talking about, and it was technically beyond my under-standing much of it, because I am not a forester. But it's a very valid concept. That's probably only one of many opportunities.

We are doing some things here. For years it was thought that the greenback trout, the greenback cutthroat, was extinct. It is the only native trout to the Platte River system, which we're a part of on the east side of the park. For years, it was thought that maybe the only remaining ones did exist here in the park, and then it was decided that there were a couple of other places where there were, in fact, pure strains. Now we have become the nucleus of re-establishing an almost extinct species. And, in fact, maybe we are the only place where it can be done successfully, because there it is. It is not the best sport fish in the world. It's too easily caught, and it is too easily wiped out. And it doesn't compete well with the non-native fishes that have been introduced. So the lobby by certain groups to prevent the state from preserving the trout is significant. You know, the state has a great deal of interest in it and has been very supportive of it. They are very limited in their ability to do it, and had the national park not been here, I suspect it would have become much more difficult to have preserved that species. So I think the national park provides some opportunities in species preservation.

The grizzly bear is another matter. Were it not for the existence of Yellowstone and Glacier National Parks, I think it would be fair to say there would be no grizzlies left in the world for man. The same would be true of bison probably. The elk herds have been re-established, and are preserved in the national parks, and then re-introduced in many cases from them.

The elk herds in the Northwest were almost all gone and they were pretty much re-established in Olympic and Mount Ranier [National Parks]. The bison was completely gone from the lower 48 of the United States, and were re-introduced from Canada into Yellowstone, and that was again the source for the redevelopment of bison herds.

It's amazing what we were able to eliminate during the 19th century. Not only were the greenback trout completely annihilated in Colorado, but so were the elk. In fact, in the 1800s the people came here for hunting and fishing and did it to such a degree and unrestrictedly that they eliminated the elk from the park, eliminated the deer and eliminated the fish. Wolf was here. Probably grizzly bear was here too at one time. I'm not sorry we don't have grizzly bears. There is a lot of interest in reintroducing wildlife, and there are also problems with it.

J: Name a few.

T: This park is — 40 percent of the boundary is private land, and within a very few years, I think that every portion of that boundary will be developed and subdivided and developed. It is proceeding so rapidly that it will be true within 10-15 years, maybe 20. Boulder County has some stricter regulations, zoning regulations on mountain property, than do the other counties, and therefore we may not have that situation on the whole strip that is in Boulder County from Long's Peak campground. But everything north of there and the east side are within that area. That presents some problems, because in that area all those people have dogs and cats and kids. They don't want wolves here regardless of facts about wolves.

J: What is the view that you would like to have of the public lands? What is your vision for them? Let's include parks as part of the mix.

T: I have difficulty looking five years into the future, with any degree of confidence. When I was in Death Valley, there was a section of the park up in the north end that, well like most of Death Valley, was pretty undeveloped, pretty wild country, even though there were lots of roads. It was still wild country. They told about a ranger that had been there — previously a district ranger — his philosophy (and he had stated it) was that he wanted, after he had completed his assignment, to go away from there with the satisfaction that his district was absolutely unchanged from the way it had been when he came there. And that certainly is one view of how things ought to be done.

  You know, the majority of people tend to think of accomplishment in terms of change. And we are in such a rapidly changing society that people need to have something that they can say, "This has not changed. This remains always the same." I think there is an inner need that people have. I don't know whether that is going to go away from us all or not. But I think it is a basic craving and I think that's something — a role — that

If I were looking a hundred years from now as a historian, or from any other period of time, that was what I would say was probably our greatest failing: our inability to look at public lands policy in the long term. And manage them for the long-term productivity, as opposed to their short-term opportunities.

James B. Thompson

the parks can fulfill. It doesn't really have to be the wild natural parks, but preserving some of the old cultural features of the country. Whether it is Mesa Verde or Grant's Tomb, I suppose.

I think there is a need to be able to go back to places and find them unchanged. That's something you can't do about your home. There are very few of us any more, particularly urban people, who are born and raised and carry out their careers and die in the same town. We all move around and when we go back to the old home, well, it's different. The house is gone. It's been replaced by a shopping mall. There are some real needs in us all to be able to go back and find something that we can remember, that we can pass on to our children. "This is what my father showed me." And I really think the only opportunities are in public ownership.

And yet, I think it is a basic strength of the people, in some ways, if you look at certain parts of the world, where tradition has really carried them through so very very much. And we really haven't had that kind of experience in this country. We haven't had the terrible things that have happened to much of the countries, only maybe the Civil War, where the civilization has almost been destroyed and the people can carry on some of the important things out of the past. I think that is the role the public lands can play. I think as the population increases that role will continue.

There is a good example here in Colorado. You know if over the next 20 years we get 800,000 more people in the Front Range, as the Governor predicts, how much that's going to change the lifestyle that all of us experience. And yet, the lifestyle is one of the greatest attractions to living in this part of the country.

I really can't look 100 years ahead, but if I could and if I was thinking about my great-great-grandchildren, who will be living 100 years from now, there are certainly some things that I hope they would see that will be very different, most of which I wouldn't care to articulate. But there are some things that I would like to have them see that remain the same. And I think that is the role the public lands play.

J: If your great-great-grandchildren . . . talking one hundred
years from now, looking back at our generation today, as historians, or as you or I might sit and look back at 1885, how
would we judge or assess our public land policies? What would
people say about our management of the public lands today?

T: Policy is something that changes overnight. And/or at least
relatively rapidly. And I'm not sure I even know what our public
lands policy is today. If you look at public lands policy over the
long term, I think it has varied from a sense of stewardship to a
sense of expediency — "Now is the time to accomplish this" —
and it goes both ways. I think there have been times when we
have moved too quickly in one direction or the other. Policies
change too rapidly.

   If I were looking a hundred years from now as a historian,
or from any other period of time, that was what I would say was
probably our greatest failing: our inability to look at public lands
policy in the long term. And manage them for the long-term productivity, as opposed to their short-term opportunities. I would
hope, on the other hand, that we can look back and say a hundred years from now that some of the options that are available to
people in that day, are available because of our public land policies today, because of our management of them, and to what degree it is available, because of our consistency. The inconsisten-
cies are our greatest failing, but if we succeed in preserving
those options for the future, it will be because we have been relatively consistent in direction.

   I think that there have been some significant accomplishments in the last 20 years. In doing just that — in setting a
direction and preserving some options, coming closer together in
our ability to define long-term productivity. The Forest Service,
BLM, National Park Service, other land managers, ranchers,
tenant harvesters, have always had differences in what we are
doing, but there is a common language that didn't exist maybe
25 years ago. And the Federal Land Management Policy Act
brought a number of those things together, common ways of
looking at things, even though it can be argued that it is

time-consuming and with a lot of bureaucratic stuff involved in it. It is as aggravating to me at times as it is to other people. Nonetheless, those are some significant accomplishments, I think, in developing a more consistent public lands policy.

Now if you want to look at some of the most bizarre periods, ups and downs, in public land use, look at World War II, when lands were open to grazing, to mining, to military operations, training grounds — everything was justified on the basis of war, of national security. Everything that anybody wanted to do on public lands, for 20 to 30 years, hadn't been allowed to do, suddenly became an issue of national security, and those were the kinds of opportunistic zig-zags in public land policy that I think came about. Maybe they were necessary, maybe the damage wasn't that great, but that wasn't the reason.

Grazing was permitted in a number of parks. Mining was permitted in a number of parks; grazing was extended in some. Grazing particularly. Even though President Roosevelt and Secretary Hickey were really very strong in their desire to protect the parks. It is interesting. The situation in the park establishment, confirms that that was certainly an intent. We have achieved a lot of those things in the long run, in 70 years — this is our 70th year anniversary. Many of those specific intrusions, as they say, have been removed. A number of them are still there, and we have acquired properties with a life tenancy where the property owner can stay there the rest of their life, or 25 years or something like that. And when they leave that particular unnatural intrusion, the man-made intrusion can be removed. In that sense, that's the long run. In the long run, it is okay to say, "All right; we will pay a little less for this property and let them stay a little longer. But in the long run, it will accomplish our objective." And I suppose in that sense, that's a case where the long term is served well — by short term expediency, if you will.

June 1985
Rocky Mountain National Park, Colorado

CARL BAGGE ————————————————————

Carl Bagge is President of the National Coal Association. His view is representative of the coal industry as a whole, although realistically, there is a variety of views among individual members. The National Coal Association represents its members in Washington as their special interest lobby.

JUNKIN: How do you view the public lands of the west? What do you perceive to be the value of the lands?

BAGGE: Well, the value of the public lands lies, it seems to me, in the ability of our political system to put them to productive use for our society. You know, other than that, there may be some psychic value from having them, but if we are talking about resources, I think their value to our society only exists to the extent to which we can create a mechanism that will make them available for use of the public. You know, that's my view of it.

J: That's exactly what I want — your view. What is, in your opinion, the best use for the public lands?

B: Well, I think I answered that with the first one. I think you know with all the grief Jim Watt took, his underlying philosophy was to put the lands in a position where they can be used for the benefit of the public. You know, it is as simple as that.

J: What should the public look to the public lands for in the future — 30, 50, 100 years out?

B: To provide the resource, the space, to keep the system going — that's what we're talking about. At the coal seminar here, we're showing that we haven't even developed a national consensus on how we will go about doing that. We are all hung up with short-term proprietary interest, trying to maximize short term moneys for the government as opposed to long-term realization of income for the government, plus benefits to the public.

But we haven't even developed a national consensus. That's why we are having all of these problems with respect to the mechanism by which we establish a simple coal leasing policy, and we are all hung up on that. There may be religious and ecological overtones we are trying to come to grips with. Why is it that in every other area of our economy, we are looking toward a market-oriented resolution of these problems, and yet when it comes to a resource like coal, we can be so critical of the electric utility rate payers in the nation? We are all hung up on philosophical grounds that we can't define yet, which prevent us from making rational judgments to create a consensus, to create a mechanism which is going to try to accommodate all the different values that are involved in that decision.

J: Let's look at the lands a hundred years in the future.

B: A hundred years? I can't look a hundred years in the future.

J: But somebody had to look ahead two hundred years as they created this country, so let's try. If you were to close your eyes and you could paint a picture of the lands, what would be the view, what would be the picture you would want to have of the public lands in the west?

B: I can't even — I'm not smart enough to even imagine 100 years from now. You know, I've got to beg off on that one. I am not a futurist. You've got to get some future nut to tell you about that. I can't deal with that.

J: Okay. Let's try the other direction. Go a hundred years into the future and look back at our generation today, as historians might. What would we say about our public land policy and natural resource policy?

B: I think they are tragic. I think it is tragic, because politics — instead of sound economics — politics have dominated the dialogue and therefore it is extremely difficult to provide any

*T*he value of the public lands
lie, it seems to me, in the ability of our political system to put
them to productive use for our society.

Carl Bagge

rational analysis of the whole program. You know, I look at it from the point of view of the coal industry, but I am sure it is also true with the other resources.

Well, look back ten years. I won't say 100 years. Take what occurred with respect again to coal — again, that is the only thing that I pray over, that I am worried about, that I am paid to pray over. I was sitting at that time on the Federal Park Commission. We had pending before us a whole series of license applications to dam the Colorado [River] because the next increment of power for the American West, or at least the southwest with the expansion of California and the whole southwest — we were struggling to see how we were going to meet that next increment of massive power generation. One option for us nationally was to take our water resources and dam the Colorado. Well, that got translated in the public mind as somehow impinging on the Grand Canyon, which was sacrosanct and we had all sorts of political pressures on us not to license dams on the Colorado — although in fact there were no dams proposed within the boundaries of the Grand Canyon National Park, or even close to it. So that was politically rejected.

We then had the second option of dedicating from nine to twelve billion dollars worth of natural gas, specifically the King Ranch resources that were under lease by Exxon. It was the so-called Gulf-Pacific case to take the next increment of power for electric power generation by natural gas. That happened to be before us also, because we regulated at that time, of course, the certification of all the natural gas pipelines and we rejected that by a two to three vote. I voted against it at the time, not even thinking about the rationality or the irrationality of using natural gas as a boiler fuel to commit the consumers of Southern California Edison for the next 50 years to natural gas. We denied that, but really for the wrong reason. I mean our instincts were good, it was to protect the gas consumers of the southwest. Following that, we had a big gas shortage and then we suddenly got the wisdom that maybe it wasn't sound national policy to be committing billions of million cubic feet of natural gas to electric power generation.

Well, we did it for the wrong reason, but it turned out to be the right decision. At that time, and now I am talking about the decade of the 1960s and not a hundred years in the past, having rejected the hydroelectric option for environmental and religious reasons, and having rejected natural gas because of consumer interests, although in retrospect, it would have been irrational to do that, then we embarked for the first time in a massive program of coal leasing. But Stuart Udall, who was then the Secretary of the Interior — whom we dealt with even though we were an independent regulatory body — Stuart Udall and the Johnson Administration wanted to give employment to the Indians. And that was, I think in political terms, probably the chief motivating factor that triggered the leasing of western coal. No one anticipated the oil embargo. Nobody anticipated the explosion of western coal. I remember vividly in the Gulf-Pacific Oil argument before the Federal Power Commission, the coal interests were there and had a map showing all this coal. This is where it is going to be, we sort of snickered at the thought of that coal providing the next power for the American southwest. Well, it did do precisely that.

The point is, you can't predict. I mean, you know ten years ago, nuclear power was going to be too cheap to meter and coal was relegated to the scrap heap. The electrical utility industry said after the building of the first Oyster Creek Nuclear Plant in New Jersey, that never again would there be another coal-fired, fossil fuel plant built in the United States, because the cost of nuclear energy was so cheap.

So you can't look 100 years. You can't even look 15 years. Of course, the 16 billion tons of coal that were under lease then provided the hysteria following the Johnson Administration, when you had a Republican administration and you had a Republic Secretary of Interior in the form of Rogers Morton. Well, Rogers Morton had to take all the heat on this sale in the previous administration — 16 billion tons of coal by leases.

Leases are only an option to development. A press release was issued in 1971 imposing a moratorium on coal leasing, and for 10 to12 years, we have been struggling with that thing ever since. So you can't make any predictions. Nuclear power versus coal — who knows what the future will hold. You can't really predict.

But the importance of what we have learned I think, or what we should have learned is that if we hadn't leased coal in the 1960s, looking at it after the oil embargo and after the enactment of the Clean Air Act and after the explosion of the Western Coal Development, we, as a society, would not have been in a position to put our enterprise system to work in accommodating that new need.

So all I am saying is that we should have learned from that — that having a proprietary view of natural resources, while the government tries to exact the greatest amount of economic rent up front by bidding and all that — really doesn't make much sense in terms of the public policy. We should have learned from that, and yet we are still too involved in the rhetoric and the politics of forging a consensus on how we go about it.

J: Who should speak for the public lands? Are you saying that with a proprietary view of natural resources — even on public lands — private industry should speak first?

B: Well, we've got enough laws on the books now that provide a variety of participants. It is not just your legislators in Congress, but it is the state, the Governor, too. We have got that apparatus set up, and even after having set up the apparatus, we still have frustrations, those of us who are trying to take a gamble. All a coal lease is, is a dice roll, because all you are given is a window of opportunity for ten years. And because of diligence, if you haven't found your market and developed one percent of the resource in ten years, you will lose the lease. So we are being forced as co-producers to take a roll of the dice.

It is not surprising at all to me that there aren't a lot of participants in coal leasing when the leases come about, because you are subject to a philosophy that attempts to exact from you the greatest price up front, where the public may well be benefited by not trying to exact that. The real increment of financial money flowing to the federal treasury comes from the development of that coal resource because of the royalty payments and because of everything else — not from the so-called bargain basement prices under Jim Watt. But the hysteria surrounding that led to a lot of misunderstanding, and so we can't get from here to there.

Today you've got a whole variety — I mean there isn't anybody who can't speak for the public lands by law. So it's a multi-interest group process already. And even with that in place, we can't arrive at a consensus.

We've got these laws on the books and there shouldn't be any more demagoguery about a lot of these issues. It saddens me to see that we are acting as though none of these laws — the Surface Mine Reclamation Act, for example, or all of these pervasive laws that radically altered the way we go about as a society in making a resource available — as if none of these laws weren't passed. It saddens me.

May 1985
Denver, Colorado

BOB FERRIS

Bob Ferris is a retired career National Park Service ranger. He started his service in Platte National Park in Oklahoma. He served seven years at Olympic National Park. We talked while we were both playing "tourist" on the train to Denali National Park in Alaska.

FERRIS: They have this use philosophy — man thinks that everything has to be used — they want to use the lava — but what use is that? Why can't it just sit there. Someone once said to me, "What good is the Olympic Peninsula? There are all those trees and no one can use them?" Well, just knowing it's there.

JUNKIN: Is that how you describe the value of the public lands to people who may not ever see the majority of these lands?

I'd say the best use is what
would be best for the country as a whole. And I'd say that
goes beyond public lands and I would include farm lands in
the mid-west because we are losing our soil at four to five
billion tons a year, and the whole future of the nation
depends on that soil. Without that, we're done.We're going
to become a second rate nation — it's going to happen. We
have this philosophy, the government can't tell the people
what to do with their land. But it's not really their land, it's
everybody's land, because we all survive on it and our
future generations survive on it — from use of the land.
When it goes, we're just going to be down the drain.

Bob Ferris

F: When you say the value, the first thing they think of is the value to whom? To us. And I just think of us — man — as part of nature, as part of the earth, not everything *for* us. We're not much different from the chipmunks or the caribou. We're all part of the biosphere. Everything is not here for us — that's contrary to a lot of religious beliefs. Maybe it's closest to the Buddhists.

J: What's the best use for the public lands? How do we define it?

F: Well, now we're getting back to people again and more logic-al. I'd say the best use is what would be best for the country as a whole. And I'd say that goes beyond public lands and I would include farm lands in the mid-west because we are losing our soil at four to five billion tons a year, and the whole future of the na-tion depends on that soil. Without that, we're done. We're going to become a second rate nation — it's going to happen. We have this philosophy, the government can't tell the people what to do with their land. But it's not really their land, it's everybody's land, because we all survive on it and our future generations sur-vive on it — from use of the land. When it goes, we're just going to be down the drain. That's more important than any ideology.

J: Is there a best use we can define?

F: I would define it as best for the public and the country, and not what is best for the vested special interest groups.

J: What will be the purpose of the lands in the future? What should we look to them for?

F: Sustenance, for the future generations, and the quality of life. We don't like to see people everywhere we go — like Mount Whitney. You see people on the trail whenever you hike; it's overdone.

It's one of the hardest things to tell people "Don't" in the national parks. You don't want to say don't do this, don't do that. You feel silly, you hate to tell them to leave the rocks and things alone. But there are reasons to, like in Arches National Monument — it's a park now — there were little red rocks called chirt — they were nice and shiny — and there was a whole hillside of them. People would dig them up and take them home with them — a whole hillside of rocks disappeared — where before, people could see them in the sunlight and it shone — so they took it home and threw it away, most likely. It just scattered and disappeared. But people couldn't understand why they couldn't take a little rock. I would explain that to them. But sometimes, they'd take dinosaur bones and fossils anyway. The wildflowers — each flower has a lot of seeds that would become others — and people don't think about that.

J: I'm trying to get people to think about the future of the land. If we looked 100 years in the future, what would you like to see on the public lands? What would you want to see change from what we see today? How would you describe it to someone?

F: I would like to see not too much changed. I would like to see them still public — and they may not be. I would like to see rational use of the land for all the people, just another way of saying what I said before. The main thing is I think we should think of the future generations between now and a hundred years. It's important to us to think of them, because we'll be gone and they'll be here, and they'll hate us if we destroy their legacy.

J: If we were a hundred years in the future looking back at today, what would we say about our management?

F: Oh, we'd be a better people if we progress in our thinking, is what I think. This is subjective, you know. We'd look back at this time and think what a bunch of mallet-heads. What was the matter with those people, with the way they handled it? We'd know too, that some people were dedicated, and that there was

this controversy. Some people you can't reach — like loggers.
You just can't reach them. They want to use everything up. They
say, "What good is it if you don't use it?" Yeah — they always
say "this over-mature harvest." They never planted it, so how
can you harvest something you didn't plant. This is a concept,
you see. They "harvest" wildlife. They harvest the wildlife, going out and shooting the birds. I'm not against hunting, don't
get me wrong — but they call it a harvest. How can they harvest
something, they didn't plant?

J: What would you change? If you think we would be sorry a
hundred years from now for what we're doing today, what
should we change?

F: Well, one of the things we would change is development. I
don't know about these parks up here in Alaska — but in the
ones in the lower forty-eight, there's a strong tendency for local
entrepreneurs, merchants and towns adjacent to the parks to want
to lure the tourist, and in order to do that, they have to have more
roads, more development. They would make Coney Islands out
of a lot of parks just to get the tourist dollar and they don't care.
That's one of the reasons we're getting the parks is because of
the tourist dollar and a lot of people have no concept of what a
park should be.

Those attitudes, I think. It's the attitudes I'd like to change
. . . if I was a hundred years from now reading back as to what
we were like. But then, maybe a hundred years from now,
maybe we won't be as advanced — maybe we will have
regressed. Who knows?

September 1985
Denali National Park, Alaska

DAVID GETCHES _____

David Getches is Executive Director of the Colorado State Department of Natural Resources. He is also an environmental lawyer and professor at the University of Colorado Law School.

_____

GETCHES: The lands are valuable for different things to different people. They have been known first for their commodity values. Our policy, of course, in the early years of the nation was to dispose of and to plunder the lands, and I don't say that cavalierly. It was a policy of plunder. Private industries were allowed to come in and exploit the lands further, and it was really only around the turn of the century that we adopted the philosophy that some of those lands should be retained for the long-term public good. That philosophy is still with us today, with some dissenters.

The idea of retention of the public land is one that excites people for a variety of different reasons. It is something of a trust fund of a capital asset, and we understand the capital asset not to be just one that we will derive income from in the economic sense, but to derive psychic income from — knowing it is there. People in New Jersey are very defensive of disposing or exploiting in a ruinous way, the land in Alaska that they have never seen. So it is this sort of inherent public land spirit that is in the American breast, if you will. It just is a feeling that it is part of our natural heritage that has been passed on to our children. It is our legacy and it will be our legacy to our children. It is something that separates the United States from other countries, in that we have at first taken it for granted and now have defended that kind of heritage.

You know, even a Libertarian admits there is a proper role of government in some areas, say national defense, or road building. I think that we find a number of Libertarians in the United States defending the maintenance and protection of the public lands as a proper function. Now they draw different lines as to what they would keep and what they would get rid of. John

Baden, of Montana State University, would say that we should
sell off the parks and privatize them. I have some problems with
that, but I think that whatever it is — whether it is wilderness or
a national forest or some BLM lands that are valuable for grazing
— and now we find the plant populations or communities that
exist no place else in the world — to maintain animal habitats is
something that people will vigorously defend.

JUNKIN: Is it your perception that this feeling of heritage is still
within the public, or is it something that needs to be rekindled?

G: I think it ebbs and flows, but rather ironically I think that
Americans have been awakened and sensitized to the need for
public lands. Their heritage that is connected with the public
lands — not so much by reason or by some reasoned temperance
that has moved them, but rather by the outrages of Jim Watt, and
by an incipient public land policy that has threatened, at least
through their rhetorical hyperbola, our national heritage. A lot of
people had never thought about public land policy until the picture of Jim Watt was flashed across the cover of *Newsweek* mag-
azine, and people realized that there is something out there that
they care for that was being threatened.

J: How can we describe the best use of the public lands? What is
going to be their purpose in the future?

G: Well, I think that there is a variety of purposes and I hesitate
to lapse into the jargon of multiple use, but I think that it is a very
good way to capture my view and what I think is the common national view of the public lands. There are all kinds of land out
there — if we are going to preserve some. We have already dis-
posed of 98 percent of what we started with. We have to be flex-
ible in how we use those lands. Some lands are valuable primarily for preserving a reserve of oil and gas or coal. Some of those
lands are valuable primarily for wilderness.

We are finding now through studies recently completed at
Colorado State University that people are willing to pay just to

know the wilderness is there, in case they want to look at it or in case they don't. They are just willing to pay, at least in Colorado, $19.00 per family just for the preservation of all the wilderness. That adds up to a lot of money. I have the summary on that because I was asked to do a report on the value of wilderness in Colorado. How much is it worth to you? Some of those public lands are particularly valuable for timber. We are in a big debate here about what Colorado forests are mostly valuable for. We find ourselves caught in a tide of national policy, that says more timber should be developed, ironically when there is a glut on the market, and private timberlands aren't being cut because there is not a market. We think the trees in Colorado that take 200 years to reach maturity, by and large should not be part of our market. I guess there are some forests that are being in Colorado, but in the mountains, the primary use for the forest is recreation. That's an illustration I think, of how we have got to be flexible with multiple use. It doesn't mean when you have forest, you set national cutting goals; it means that you take a very sensitive approach that personalizes each parcel of public land, and find what its very best uses are. And by best, I mean public economic sense, not just what we can derive a short term profit from. How would we want to invest these public lands is the question. They are an asset. And if we want to invest them in a quick-profit return, we have to ask what do we give up? Is there a price to the resources later? Do we give up some opportunity value that we have?

For example, look at an area that could be a campground or backpacking area for the next two centuries. What is that worth versus the value sacrificed by strip mining it, or cutting the timber? I think there are many times we make the decision: let's cut the timber, let's take out the minerals. Sometimes it is not inconsistent. I think that people are shortsighted if they take the view that every bit should be totally preserved or every inch of it should be strip-mined.

J: Let's take a look 100 years in the future. What is it you would like to see? What is your vision?

So I guess what I would like to see is the maturing of that management so that we really do have management that is close to the land, that understands, that is informed of the values of each parcel and will not be set aside by some distant policy setter . . .

I think that it is somewhat disappointing to me that we don't get to look 100 years into the futures. I just returned from a legislative battle over ground water, and there I'm trying to get the legislature to look 100 or 200 or 1000 years into the future and they refuse to do it.

David Getches

G: I guess the difference I would like to see would be in an approach of management. I don't think we are far off the mark in having about the right amount of public lands, and I think that we are approaching the designation of them for particular uses in reasonable ways. But I think we have to make some thoughtful changes in management. We have to have more response to the things that a particular area of the public lands are most valuable for, instead of having broad national policies: that they cut x percent timber in each and every forest mentality. We are planning for the national forests. Unfortunately the cutting plans are driven from the top down, from the chief's office in Washington, instead of being what the architects of the National Forest Management Act envisioned — and that is a carefully developed plan that is peculiar to each forest. So I guess what I would like to see is the maturing of that management so that we really do have management that is close to the land, that understands, that is informed of the values of each parcel and will not be set aside by some distant policy-setter.

I think you should not look for any great acquisitions, and other than doing away with a hotel in Waikiki, or whatever the examples of privatization are, I don't think we ought to look for any major disposals either. Exchanges are good; I think that we can do a lot to consolidate lands, to get rid of in-holdings to take the uneconomic ions of public land that are out someplace in the middle of private lands and exchange them. There could be a lot of benefit from exchanges of state public land and private land. Although I agree with the waves of laws that came in the mid-70s and I also agree with what drove those laws, there is some very provocative litigation over the public lands. There never was litigation over the public lands, until probably it started in the '60s. I think lawyers felt their oats, and people felt that lawyers could answer a lot of questions. They watched it work in the civil rights arena and because it worked in civil rights, they were driven to do something in the public land and environmental arena, and it really did work there. But I think that has peaked out. Now we have laws in place that impose these rigorous management requirements.

I think part of the answer is following through with those management requirements but also relaxing some of them, and that might surprise you as part of my answer. I think that right now that the Forest Service and the BLM and these other land management agencies are becoming hamstrung by regulations. They are drowning in paperwork. And if they are going to follow through with the intent of those laws and personalize the management to the states that they are dealing with, they will have to be given more flexibility. That means they have to be given some power to stand up against the mining company, or on the other hand, somebody who has an unreasonable approach to preservation. They have to strike an appropriate balance, and they have to believe in the lands in their heart, and then you have to trust them a little bit at the local level.

J: We have to personalize management both for good and bad at the state and/or regional level?

G: Yes, I think regional level, state level, forest level, and sometimes it crosses state lines. I think without appearing to get into the mind set of the Sagebrush Rebellion, I do think the states have a real role in how the public lands are managed. I think that this is a philosophy of mine that my colleagues disagree on. I think the states and local government should be able to zone public lands and to limit land use. I don't think they ought to be able, of course, to develop it, but it ought to be just like private land.

I have property in the mountains. You can't force me to develop, but you can force me not to put in a mine where the county doesn't want it. I think that would be a reasonable approach to managing the public lands; it is very revolutionary, but why should we treat those federal lands that differently? It's probably preservation-oriented in its outcome.

J: How would you judge what you are doing today in your office? Let's look a hundred years into the future.

G: I think that it is somewhat disappointing to me that we don't get to look 100 years into the future. I just returned from a legislative battle over ground water, and there I'm trying to get the legislature to look 100 or 200 or 1000 years into the future and they refuse to do it. Colorado is notorious in its resistance to any kind of long range plan, as it affects land.

Counties and cities do planning, but the state had better not touch that issue. I think that is a very disappointing attitude. Somebody ought to be taking the long look. Our failure to take the long look I think forecloses a lot of opportunities for our children. There are times when we look to government to exert restraint on us that we would like to be able to exert if we had the statesmanship or the discipline to do it ourselves, and that is another role, I suppose, for higher levels of government, like the federal government, and the state.

June 1985
Denver, Colorado

WARD REDFORD _____

Ward Redford is a conductor on the Alaska Railroad. He is also a folk naturalist and a wildlife photographer. He has lived twenty of his twenty-eight years in Alaska and considers the state his home. We spoke while on the Railroad trip to Denali National Park.

JUNKIN: How would you describe the value of all of this?

REDFORD: The value. Talk about a dollar value, there is none. I mean, it's just out of sight. The value for the public lands that we have here in Alaska is being able to get away from it all — from the concrete jungles. I really don't know how to put it — but it's the peace you find there. It's just you and me and the wolf. And its basically still untouched by humans here in Alaska. It really is. Even in Denali Park, with its 400,000 people per year going through it. If you stay right on the road you can see the signs of civilization. If you are willing to hike, you can go back in, like I do, you can walk over ground that humans have never walked over. And it's just mind-boggling to me, the space is. To someone that has never seen the land, or to someone who was born and raised in the city of New York, for example, I don't know how to describe it to them.

J: How would you describe the purpose of having them if someone's never going to see them?

R: There are people, I know by the number of people I talk to, who live in big cities who are interested in these lands. Two summers ago, I had a couple I took back into the park with me, and they were wildlife majors in college, and a moose got within thirty feet of us. The moose, she walked up on us. It totally blew the couple's mind. They were used to seeing them in a zoo or whatever. So the value of the land is there, whether they are going to come and see it or not . . . to some people. Other people couldn't care less. But I think that to the biggest portion of the country, there is a great value in keeping the land as it is.

I don't want our national parks and preserves to become like Yellowstone National Park. I don't know how to prevent it, because everybody has the right to see it, but on the other hand   . . . Fortunately, we are far enough away that we don't get the millions of visitors. But I really wish they could see it, too. To me, the land that we have that I use, that is public, is extremely valuable.

J: What is the "best use" for it?

W: That's a delicate question on the balance of use. I'm not an environmentalist. On the other hand, I don't want to strip it all either. I realize that we have to have the oil. We have to have the other minerals that are there. The question is, how do we accomplish everybody's goals to the greatest value for all? Here in

I don't want our national parks and preserves to become like Yellowstone National Park. I don't know how to prevent it, because everybody has the right to see it, but on the other hand . . . Fortunately, we are far enough away that we don't get the millions of visitors.

Ward Redford

Alaska, some of our preserves are open to mining and to other
things. I don't mind that, as long as they restore it. I could take
you up here to a strip mine near McKinley Park who spent his
own money to reclaim the land. He reseeded it for Dall sheep.
It's probably better now than it was originally. On the other
hand, I've seen some mines from a hundred years ago and it still
shows. I don't like that.

Best use of the land? It's got to be a balance. I think the miners should be able to use the public land, but I also think someone should be there to return it to how they found it. Or maybe
make it better. Think about the wildlife in the area when you reclaim it. I guess the best use of public lands, to me, would be a
balance. And then if they did allow development, then they
should put it back. But I think we do need some land — some
we don't need to tear up at all. Some we should just leave the
way it is, and let nature do its thing to it and leave it.

J: What is your vision for the public lands? If we were to look a
hundred years from now at what we see from this train, what
would you like to see?

R: A hundred years from now? I'd like to be able to say that it
would be like it was fifty years ago. That's a dream. This country fifty years ago — or even twenty years ago when I came up
— it was almost impossible to take a short drive from town and
not see wildlife. Now it's rare. Back when I was younger, I did
a lot of hunting — I don't do it anymore — and if I couldn't take
my moose an hour from my house, I wouldn't bother. And now,
that's rare. I would like to step back in time, if I could, but I
know I couldn't. So basically my real goal for a hundred years
from now is to have it just like it is.

I don't agree with the BLM and the Park Service and the
Forest Service; we've got too many people controlling the lands.
That would be one thing I would like to change. We need a Department of Interior — or I don't care who. But we need one person who has control over all the land. Not the way it is, with the

Fish and Wildlife here and the Park Service there and the BLM
and Forest Service, because they don't — and won't — work
together. The U.S. government agencies won't work together.
Even the Forest Service and the Park Service don't work together, so I'd like to see them consolidate all the public lands into
one heading, so they all answer to the same person, but not way
up the ladder like it is now.

J: If from a hundred years in the future, we looked back, what
would we say about our land management today?

R: I think we are at a changing point here. I think they'd look
back and say we wiped out the biggest portion of it. I really feel
people are changing now, and that we have a chance for making
it the same as it was. But if we looked back, I'd say that we
wiped out the best parts of it. That's simply how I feel.

J: Feeling that, what would you change, if you could?

R: I don't know if we can change anything because of the al-
mighty dollar. Some people don't give a ripp, as long as there's
a dollar involved. Some people don't care what they do, they'll
do anything for a dollar. The best way to change it is to start in
the school system. By the time you're an adult, you're not going
to change. Maybe forty years ago, we had maybe 80, 90 thousand people living in the state and 186,000 square miles of land.
Now Anchorage has 225,000 right there in one town. When you
only have 80 or 90 thousand people and all that land, you could
pretty much do as you please. We used it, but we didn't tear it
up. You can't let just everybody use it that way anymore, the
way they want. Like I don't like the fact in Denali that you can't
drive your own vehicle in. But then I see pictures of Yellowstone, and I don't want that. So maybe it's best that you can
drive in after Labor Day and before Memorial Day, but even
that's getting bad. I would like to see Denali Park with another
road in — not another asphalt road, but a dirt road, and not one
that connects, because then people will do a loop.

J: Do you see a value in a place like Lake Clark National Park, where the only way to get in is to fly?

R: We need some of that land where there is limited access. It does allow some people like myself who totally like to get away from it. It's extremely expensive — you have to fly in — but there are people who want that and who will pay for it. I don't feel like we are gypping anyone else as long as we have an excess of space like in Denali Park or in the state parks, or near Anchorage. Within twenty minutes of my house, I'm in the forest. So there's no complaints about Lake Clark because there are other options. I do not think that just because it is public land, we have to have access to it. I do not think we need access to every place. Gateway to the Arctic — beautiful place — if they start building roads into there, I'll be screaming wild, because, as I said, I don't want Yellowstones, if we can avoid it.

J: In 1872, they had no idea that Yellowstone would become so crowded as it is today. What's to prevent the same in Alaska?

R: Every year, it's more and more and more people. When I first started researching the park borders, it was only 200,000 people per year. I bet it's up to half a million, so it's a long ways a way from what Yellowstone sees. But it's still only three to five hours away from most other parts of the lower 48 country. It's expensive, but there will be more and more people. Another idea I'd like to see is to make another access train only — run them slower, avoid the busses — because we need a little more access to the park to spread out the impact — we won't hurt anything with a little more access.

September 1985
Denali National Park

JAY HAMMOND _____

Jay Hammond was Governor of Alaska during the debate over the Alaska Lands Act in 1980. He arrived in Alaska in 1946. He took the unpopular and politically difficult path of advocating a different form of land management than either private interests (a land grab) or environmentalists (setting aside of more land) wanted. He has argued for cooperative management." If the most stringent preservation standards were compromised a bit, other resource standards would be raised. The result would be, he thought, that a higher standard of environmental preservation could be maintained throughout the state, rather than the patchwork standards and management that exists in the "lower 48." Unfortunately, he believes, no one really listened to what he was saying and the entire debate became captive of jargon, catch words like wilderness, multiple use and park protections, rather than sitting down and realizing that there was, in large part, agreement as to the high standard of protection that was desired. Governor Hammond has since "retired" from politics, returning to live in the bush around Lake Clark National Park.

_____

HAMMOND: People seek certain wilderness considerations, which, if you make them available to too great a number, you've automatically altered them in such a way to make them no longer appealing. It's a difficult thing to describe those values or a balance that are found on public lands or are available in a greater degree than elsewhere.

JUNKIN: Is there a "best use?" How do we describe it?

H: The best use is to retain them, I suppose, to provide the greatest benefit or satisfaction to the greatest number of people. Again, you reach a point of diminishing returns. You've got the Yellowstone syndrome there — more and more people flood in, less and less there is to enjoy. And yet, is it better to provide for an elite few an enormous, 100 percent value experience, or to provide for a multitude a fifty percent value experience? Well, of course, for the elite few — and I consider myself one of the fortunate who have experienced the one hundred percent value — that's a diminishment. And yet, on the other hand, to the individ-

ual who never had the opportunity to do any of that, you're ele-
vating to a fifty percent experience is a hard thing to call.

Of course, I'd like the country much better back in the hills,
if it were forty years ago. It was 72,000 people up here then and
I thought it was a little crowded. Now there are 500,000 and it's
teeming to me, but again, there are many more people who are
seeing and I hope appreciating public lands resource values that
were here back then. I suppose that is "better" than the elitist position I was fortunate enough to participate in, but I have to admit
a certain sorrow associated with its no longer being available.

J: It's an interesting question to me about Lake Clark National
Park — it is difficult to get to and thus is a different sort of public land. One of the rangers there said something to the effect of,
"Look, just because it's public land doesn't mean you, the public, have to have access." Would you agree that land simply held
as public land, without easy access, has a value? Could we try to
describe that to the public who is being kept out?

H: At one time, they wanted to put a road down through Lake
Clark Pass, and I was in the legislature at the time, and frankly,
it didn't make sense. There were glaciers across and it would
have been enormously expensive. Had they initiated it, it probably would have been done, because once they start down those
trails, they find someway to continue to throw good money after
bad. It was one of those things that got me cross-sighted with
some conservationists.

I suggested that if you have to put a road down across the
Alaska Peninsula — this is where the cooperative management
concept comes into play — because we don't consider putting a
road through the park, the much more logical, least environmentally damaging route, the least costly route was foreclosed. So
by default they were going to go through a by-far more damaging area, but it wasn't in a "park," but as far as doing violence
to habitat, it was horrendous. But that is the sort of thing that
cooperative management lends itself to dealing with better.

J: What do you see as the purpose of the public lands? What should we be looking to them for? Especially in Alaska, which is so removed from the "lower 48" by transportation costs for the natural resources.

H: Well, to perpetuate, *ad infinitum*, public values. And what are public values? Public values to me are a little different in shade and coloring than they are to most people. To me, you put a road, for access or a hot dog stand, on top of a mountain, and somehow, it loses its appeal to me. Yet there are a lot of people who find that roads, or snow machine trails, or so forth, valuable. It's in the eye of the beholder. Who am I to say it is less a public value if the majority of the public favors that? I am a member of the public, but I have a different view. To me, I think they should open a fishing stream to flys only and it diminishes in value when they allow use of salmon eggs. But it's the majority of the people. The only way they will be able to fish and catch anything is to use eggs. I'm torn. Because my gut feeling is toward the elitist type of public value being enhanced over all others, yet I suppose that the greatest value is for the greatest number, as they perceive it.

J: Are you saying we should leave it to the federal agencies to decide how the public perceives public lands?

H: Well, I suppose the only way to know what the public perceives is to ask them through a vote process. But then again, I think there certainly are public values that are not clearly perceived by the public that are incredibly important. Lets say a public value might be retention of a habitat — a fish and game habitat. Well, it provides access for numbers of people. Yet you're doing violence to the very reason for the game refuge to be retained by allowing access by the people. So there is a point of diminishing return by permitting the public value which might be termed a political value — people favor it because it enhances their particular activity — over what is truly a long-term public value, which is retention of a game resource that might be

Of course in my view, the time element of immediate public value should never predominate over the long-term "public value." That is, in essence, an inheritance by the people of the generations who come behind us. Of course, the fact is that it almost always does — that's the unfortunate thing — people have let the moment prevail.

Jay Hammond

stroyed by catering to that political value of the moment. I don't
destroyed by catering to that political value of the moment. I
don't know if that makes sense to you.

J: Yes, it does. We're talking about perceptions of values and
you bring up an important question of long-term or short-term
values — how do we choose?

H: Of course in my view, the time element of immediate public
value should never predominate over the long-term "public value" that is, in essence, an inheritance by the people of the generations who come behind us. Of course, the fact is that it almost
always does — that's the unfortunate thing — people have let the
moment prevail.

J: Let's talk about the next two generations. Let's look a hundred
years from now and what would you like to see? What is your
vision for the public lands?

H: If I were here a hundred years from now, while some of my
own attitudes might have moderated or realism would have crept
in, and I recognized that you can't have it exclusively to yourself, I would still wish that there were large expanses of places
where people could still avail themselves of at least a smidgin' of
the sorts of opportunities to appreciate. The values of the public
lands, to the extent that I was privileged to do so.

It's difficult to think in terms of hundred-year values anymore, with the spectres of nuclear holocausts and things of that
nature. Not that I'm a pessimist in that regard, but I don't think
we are as inclined to look in the same depth into the crystal ball
of the future as we used to be because of those things clouding
the vision. But I, of course, think it would be tragic if we didn't
retain on the public lands the types of values that caused us to
consider them public lands, parks, refuges, wilderness experiences. If you plasticize it, pave it all over, and make it accessible
to everybody from the most simplistic, creature-comfort type, I
think you lose the appreciation for a lot of those values. You
don't appreciate things you don't have to work for in one form

or another, or pay for, and the pay may just be the sweat of your brow for having to walk up to the top of that mountain.

I remember when I came from the Adirondacks, there was a mountain there — Whiteface Mountain. They put a road up to the top of Whiteface Mountain, I remember, and there was a his and her outhouse and a hot dog stand. To me, I never cared to go back. But on the other hand, a lot of people got to see Whiteface Mountain who would have never have been able to do it. That's what troubles me; I am admittedly selfish about sharing those things. I think someone should have to work to see it and not drive through at a hundred miles per hour and not see any of the landscape. The experience they get doesn't warrant providing the facility to drive through it. But there are other people who say, "Why should it be denied me? Why can't I go up there to see it?"

Well, it seems to me there are enough things you can drive through at a hundred miles an hour. There should be a few things that require the sweat of the brow, that you have to work at, that take commitment to get to see. For example, if they put a road down to my place, I'd have no interest in living there. Now that's peculiar, but a multitude of other people would think that's great. But I would have lost the thing I found attractive.

J: Would the thing you'd like to give to your grandchildren, would it change from what we see today?

H: No. No, if I had my druthers, I'd give that same opportunity to my grandchildren. In a way, I am less concerned now about overly great access to public lands, like the Lake Clark Pass road would have provided, than I was fifteen years ago. I think the likelihood of that kind of thing occuring was much more likely under the attitude that prevailed then — "We've got to open up the country." I really think there is far less likelihood — and the Lands Act did put up some barriers that will prevent that, but I think the public attitude is less like that.

Let me give you an example: 15, 20 years ago, a lot of native communities were petitioning to get a road into Anchorage. They wanted to drive into Anchorage, get the groceries and experience all the good things civilization would bring to them. Now, they are exactly the opposite. They're opposing all the roads that go in, and so there's no longer the agitation at the state level among the political groups to put a road in. My view was that the road should come after it has evolved; you don't put it in and then wait for something to happen, assuming that this will again, make the desert bloom.

The natives have done a 180 degree reversal. I remember these people wanted a road to go into Fairbanks, from the little town of Minno. I remember telling them that they may regret it, because remember it is a two-way street. It isn't just you travelling in, and people will come the other way. Anyway, they got their road, and the first year, there was something like 200 vehicles in beautiful downtown Minno, with moose hunters and what have you, and those people screamed in anguish over what had happened to their community. It was too late. In fact, they talked about trying to blow the road up, but they didn't do it. That alerted a lot of communities to think about just how much access they want. They have seen, through just aircraft travel, an enormous change in the amount of people who invade their territory and compete for the game resources, and they have recognized that if you get a road — like the Kenai — its shoulder to shoulder like you'd see in California.

J: Have you seen it in Lake Clark with the aircraft?

H: Yes, but that's the only way to get there. I started one of the first three sport fishing operations — I was the first to do it at Lake Clark — but it was always very small — I never had more than three people over. Now they're handling fifteen — multitudes by contrast — but now there are nine lodges on Lake Clark area, and over 80 in Bristol Bay, when there used to be three. If you ask me what I'd like to see, well to me the country has changed so dramatically that I'd like to live in the past, as far as what I would aspire to. But again, what's in the "public interest?" I can't say I appreciate it as much as I used to.

J: Let's go a hundred years in the future and look back as historians at what we've done in terms of management philosophy.

H: Well, again, I find that a lot of people, when they raise a problem regarding their land management, and I mention to them this cooperative land management concept, many of them say, "Geez, why didn't we do that." I think we will find that we will do most everything that has occurred in the "lower 48." We'll duplicate the problems that they've had — the environmental degradation adjacent to these public lands — because you do not have any means of buffering other than through a tradeoff process that keeps the respective land owners out and recognizes that you've got values that extend beyond the immediate boundaries of the public lands. So, to that extent, more and more, you'll find people lamenting the fact that they didn't have a broader land use policy that encompassed other than federal lands.

I think that was one of our biggest mistakes. As the natives get under pressure, they'll divest themselves of land and you'll have private enclaves in the public lands. You're already seeing it. People are buying up the rights to fishing streams and charging fees, and you can't go here and there without paying 1500 dollars a year. Those things are lamentable and a far cry from when I came up, and it's going to get worse. No question about it. Because the natives will be under pressure to get the front money and they'll look for monetary return, they will charge or put up barriers. We've got artificial aggravation occurring, unnecessarily occurring because of statute. This subsistence is one of them. I said about subsistence — it's like the word pornography — everyone knows it when you see it, but no one can define it. It really is kind of true. When you start to make a legal definition of subsistence for hunting or fishing, you're bound to exclude some that should be included and include some that should not. To me, they've gone about that all wrong, too. Then, I sound like a sour old I-told-you-so-er.

On subsistence, when they created new parks, they allowed subsistence. I, by residency, am permitted to hunt in the park, despite my relatively high income and ability to acquire food stuffs without resorting to hunting. A destitute, angry native in

Anchorage cannot do that. There's something wrong with that. We could have handled it by regulating it. We could have said, "Now we don't hunt in the park because you had to walk in, or whatever, can't use an airplane to haul meat." But if we had said, "Hey if you are a qualified subsistence user, you can hunt there too, whether you live in the vicinity or not. But you don't put your goose in a plane and haul it to Anchorage. You simply sit there and eat it." No one is going to do that. But by law, they can't do it and I can and they're angry about it.

Another mistake is the local advisory committee in the area. A great agitation on the part of the locals is to try to close their area off to anyone but themselves. We need a better yardstick of subsistence. Probably the best assessment is need. And the best assessment of need is probably income. It's not great, but it works.

We were getting to a point up here a few years ago where it didn't make any difference whether you were white or native, and now its suddenly become important. Now there's aggravation on both sides and it's lamentable. It's just going to get worse as more and more of these lands are closed off to urban sportsman or sold off and people are going to get more exclusive as to who can come on.

I wish I could be optimistic. The only thing I can say is, with our decline in oil growth, I don't think we are going to muck it up as rapidly as when we had all the money in the world. I don't think we will build spaghetti networks of roads that we probably are not going to be able to use.

You ask what do I envision is going to happen? I don't think you are going to find the stimuli that attracted people to Alaska as strong as it has been the last ten years. Already they tell me that the population of Anchorage is leveling off.

I'm always on the wrong side of the popular political move — I was opposed to statehood. Don't think they didn't bump me over the head with that. I wasn't opposed to it idealistically, but I questioned our ability to finance and administer. I thought we had no income-producing industries or activities. We had such a small population, virtually anyone who aspired to public office

I think people have an innate yearning and hunger for retention of a lot of these values that they may not even be able to articulate or even think about. A lot of people don't understand why it is important to have a wilderness area out there if they are never going to be able to see it, but I think that is important. I think the frontiers of the spirit, and the mentality and the attitudes and the emotions, are as important as the physical frontiers. And just knowing that there are areas where nature and species are being retained in healthy abundance, I think, is an enormously important thing to our spiritual awareness of life in general and to our well-being. Once gone, it's diminished enormously, whether you ever get to see it or not.

Jay Hammond

could get it. We would have been absolutely belly-up without the oil. We were in terrible shape financially. We were bailed out by the earthquake and by the Fairbanks flood. They were financially the best shot in the arm. Incidently, they say five years after statehood, we lost more people from the state by every means of transportation — air or boat — than came up here. Instead of flourishing, we lost them. Fisheries were in terrible shape. Japanese competition. We really didn't have much activity.

When we got oil, we subsidized small loans, got a huge injection of people from the pipeline. I think a case can be made for cheerful pessimism — anticipate the worst and take your actions to try to offset the trauma that will occur if you ignore those things. We have not taken the actions necessary to offset the trauma, and therefore, we are exceedingly vulnerable. Public lands are likely to be altered, changed, impacted, abused, almost in direct proportion to the number of people. With fewer people, or at least a constrained population growth, from the public land point of view, it would probably be less abuse. We've seen an incredible number of people out in the hills than there used to be. I took a boat over to a little stream 25 years ago where nobody, nobody fished. Now there are six boats there, fifteen parties on the river and a big motor boat came racing up — that's because people are desperately hungry for the kinds of activities that people think Alaska can provide. The irony is that Alaska is a land of myths and misperceptions — there are so many things people believe about Alaska that aren't true.

In fact, I told this in the speech I gave today: "For example, you all know that the pipeline was delayed by the environmental preservationists. You all know that Alaska has one of the finest big-game populations of any state in the Union. You all know that Alaska's economy is one of the most healthy, that Bill Sheffield's political viability was just about squelched with the impeachment proceedings, and that any state with a liberal-socialistic program of handing checks out to the people should curtail that program before they propose to tax the people. And if you know those things, you're wrong on each and every one of them."

Take Alaska's big game population. I did an article for *Field & Stream* long about 1959 in which I found that the state of Michigan had killed 105,000 deer out of an estimated million deer population. Michigan is about one-tenth the size of Alaska. At the time, it was assumed that Alaska had about 500,000 big game animals of every type. That means that Alaska had one-twentieth of the big game per unit area. I've been far more impressed by the lack of big game, the enormous expanses of area in which there is no game in Alaska. The trouble is again, because of lack of people pressure — instead of 600,000 hunters we may only have 60,000 — but we used to only have 10,000 and that was nothing. We'd have enclaves of game in little pockets and immense areas, the size of whole states that had nothing.

J: But here we are, what can we change?

H: I don't know how we can recoup those potentials. I don't know how to stop what we've already started doing. It's like getting so many employees on the payroll: you just can't cut it, no matter what they say during the election. It's one of the faults of the political, elective office these days. I am a great advocate of one six-year term. I found in my second, lame duck administration, I was able to do a lot more moving and shaking and the public had a better sense of what I was doing because no longer did people bother to be clouded by my being a political threat. Nobody can afford to put the state interest paramount rather than their own little areas. That's one thing we could do: put a limit on political terms so people could afford to vote their conscience and know that they weren't up for re-election.

I found on the lands bill, when I was trying to propose cooperative management, I had congressmen tell me that was a great idea, but they had a consensus that they couldn't support it publicly. They'll never do anything about the deficit in Congress, because these guys have to run for re-election.

I have said many times, and it's true of lands or political issues, that to the average politician, infinity is about four years away. They can't concern themselves with ten to twenty years down the pike; it's what is going to get me re-elected. And so we pile up staggering debts or abuses, and someone else gets saddled with it later on.

I wish I could tell you something positive, but I think we've got some harsh lessons to learn, and we've laid the groundwork that almost assures we're inexorably programmed to pound our head against some of those lessons. And what shakes out in the end, I don't know. You don't spend your inheritance on your daily expenses, but we sure have.

J: How do we move toward creation of a land ethic that speaks to this ?

H: Well, the polls show that there's enormous interest in conservation issues, that it is not a passing fancy or fad. I think people have an innate yearning and hunger for retention of a lot of these values that they may not even be able to articulate or even think about. A lot of people don't understand why it is important to have a wilderness area out there if they are never going to be able to see it, but I think that is important. I think the frontiers of the spirit, and the mentality and the attitudes and the emotions, are as important as the physical frontiers. And just knowing that there are areas where nature and species are being retained in healthy abundance, I think, is an enormously important thing to our spiritual awareness of life in general and to our well-being. Once gone, it's diminished enormously, whether you ever get to see it or not.

September 1985
Lake Clark, Alaska

MARGARET MURIE _____

*Margaret Murie, known to friends and to most of Alaska as Mardy,
spent her growing-up years in Alaska. She rode the last freight line by
dog sled history would see in 1914 from her home in Fairbanks down
to the south. She married biologist Olaus Murie in the 1920s and together they spent life not only advocating protection of the environment, but living in the wild lands of this country while studying wildlife. Still working for the wilderness she has lived her life in, she
teaches classes at a field science school in Jackson, Wyoming and
writes books and articles.*

JUNKIN: What tangible or intangible values should we assign to
the public lands?

MURIE: The most important value of the public lands is that they
can be assigned intangible values. The intangible values are very
important — I think if we are looking to the future at all, we have
to assume that the people of the future are still going to be sensitive people and are going to enjoy all sorts of aesthetic experiences. We should be preserving the chance for them to have such
kinds of experiences in the future. Otherwise, we're just drop-
ping our responsibilities. Because one of the most important
things I see in young people — I deal with a great many young
people through this field science school in Jackson Hole and
other groups; I've had six or seven groups come this summer —
I think maybe the thing you can help awaken their eyes to is the
fact that if you are a citizen of this wonderful country, then you
must be willing to take some responsibility for what happens in
it. And I've been really pleased and thrilled at the response I get
from these young folks without my saying much. They come to
see me and I just try to show them how Olaus kept his notes,
kept his card files , information about animals, wildlife and wilderness. They look at his water-color drawings and read some of
the articles he wrote, and look through all of the photo albums of
all the animals, just to try to show them how an old time naturalist works and what he did later in life. And the response is, every

time this group comes in, that I don't see one disinterested face. I suppose I'm seeing the cream of the crop, because they have to have some interest in biology before they come and join in that type of group but it gives me some hope and some belief anyway. Wherever they live, they are going to be better citizens after that experience, for those six weeks in the hills around Jackson Hole, Wyoming, and getting a field science course at the same time.

J: Do you use the word "responsibility" or does that word still tend to scare people off?

M: No, I use the word. I was using that word this summer because it hit me stronger than ever that this was something that they needed to feel. And I remember one boy said," Yes, I'm going to look into what's going on when I get back to my town." I'm trying to make them believe that a lot of wonderful things can be accomplished by a few people, because history shows that — especially conservation history. My husband used to say that all the conservationists had going at that time was their stubbornness. You just don't quietly give up. And that's what happened with the Echo Park controversy, and that was the time that conservation groups learned that they had to work together. As Olaus used to say, it's going to take all of us to do it, and that's certainly true now.

J: How would we describe public lands to someone who's never going to see them — and I'm thinking of the people on the east coast who may not consider that there is so much land under federal management here.

M: I suppose we would say that public lands are lands that are, as of now, largely the way they were before white man came to this continent and so you can visualize lakes, streams, creeks, forests, forested hills, mountains. If that can help them to visualize it, that's what they are. We just hope that largely they can be kept that way — I mean I think the greatest asset for the people

The most important value of the public lands is that they can be assigned intangible values. The intangible values are very important — I think if we are looking to the future at all, we have to assume that the people of the future are still going to be sensitive people and are going to enjoy all sorts of aesthetic experiences.

Margaret Murie

of tomorrow is just leaving these lands untouched as much as possible.

J: Because of the intangible value of their simply being as it once was in this country?

M: Yes, not only the intangible value, but we don't know how many material values may come out of wilderness for the benefit of selfish man, if you want to look at it in the perfectly anthro-procentric point of view. You can say we may be saving these things because there may be a cure for cancer hidden away in the wilderness somewhere. The cure for malaria and tuberculosis came out of the wilderness of Africa. Yes, the abalone has some quality that is effective in the treatment of mastoiditis — and that's just the beginning. Nobody knows how many more there may be for the future. So, we're just trying to be unselfish in our thinking of how we treat the public lands.

And of course, we're very much concerned about how our national forests are being treated. It's such a vital, hot issue right now. I know a lot of my dear Forest Service friends feel they're being trampled on now — with deficit timber sales and the thing that goes with them — the road building, which is even more of a concern as far as wildlife is concerned, and we're in the midst of all that.

J: There is always talk about "best use" of public lands — it's part of the jargon of public land policy. I wonder what you would say is the best use of the public lands?

M: Well, of course, you probably expected me to say that the best use for most of the public lands is to not use them — because of these things I've just mentioned. There are benefits for man hidden away there. The other thing is the people of the future may still be sensitive and receptive enough that they can need, use and enjoy lands that are still fairly natural. I feel it should be a part of our civilization and we are lacking in our responsibilities if we don't make some effort to keep it that way.

J: We've talked a little bit already about what purpose the lands will serve in the future. So let's try to look a hundred years into the future. Jefferson must have had some kind of vision for the land. How could any president today make a purchase of totally inaccessible lands with more money than was in the treasury and then have the nerve to tell the people that he did it for their benefit? I couldn't imagine someone doing it today.

M: He was a brave man and I wonder if he really knew what he was doing?

J: If we could look a hundred years into the future, what is the view that you would like to have of the public lands? What would you actually see, if we looked out from Jackson or Moose, or Anchorage?

M: I think I hope we could still see forested hills and craggy mountains and snow-capped mountains and streams that are not running with mud and lakes that are not being polluted. I don't see any good reason why we can't have those things if we wake up right now to the fact that these lands warrant some very careful stewardship. If we don't give it that stewardship, then we are failing in our responsibilities. I don't see why the views should not be almost the same. There are some examples in New England of some villages that are also exactly the same as they were a hundred years ago and some have been kept that way purposely. I think it's a good thing — and speaking of Thomas Jefferson, I ran across something just the other day in which he said, "A people who do not consider their past will probably not be very good caretakers of the future." So he must have been looking at the past history of our country, which wasn't very long at that point, and he must have had some feeling about what the future could be, too.

J: From that position a hundred years in the future we looked back at us sitting here today, as historians might look at our

sociey. What do you think we would say about our management
of the public lands today?

M: If we were talking about right now, today, I think we would
say, "Well, a good many things should have been more carefully
considered and there should have been more courage and wisdom about how the lands were being used at this time and more
thought for the future." I don't know how else to put it. There
are so many uses that some people think are very important —
oil and gas and timber — and they may not be so overridingly important as we may think they are. And then there's the way we're
handling the lands themselves. In agriculture, for instance, we're
probably not using the very best methods of saving the soil. I'm
sure all those tons of soil going down into the lakes and streams
— and that draining of the wet lands in South Dakota that we
heard so much about recently — all these things that are happening that shouldn't be happening. I can only hope for more courage on the part of our agencies, but you see there's sometimes
too much politics and too much pressure from various sources,
and especially from some people who see some possibility of
gain. And that's one thing I don't know what you do about. I
was interviewed by the *Wall Street Journal* once, and got into a
lot of trouble because I made the remark that I didn't know what
you could do about greed in the human heart. Some folks took
exception to that.

J: Is that what you would change if you could?

M: Yes, yes, I think it would be lovely and I think that if we had
more and more young people growing up having some such experience as they get in these camps and field science schools and
places where they are out in the public lands and national forests
and in the national parks and learning about them, it seems to me
that is about the only hope, because then the people of the future
are going to have more regard. I don't see any other way to do it;
because you're bound to be dealing with people. And then, the
other thing, the only thing we can hope is that there won't be

I'm always saying at these speeches I give that I'm a born optimist and maybe I'm an optimist because I'm a coward. Maybe I'm just not brave enough to really look the facts in the face. But even if I felt that none of these lovely things were going to take place, it would still be more interesting to me and more fun — that's what I say to these young people — it's better to be in the fight than standing in the corner with your face to the wall, no matter how it may turn out. It's better to be in it.

Margaret Murie

such a tremendous population growth that all of these lovely things will be impossible. That's the other big question.

J: You're suggesting, then, that they're a luxury, but they're also a necessity, in that we can't do without them?

M: Yes, something Newton Drury said when he was director of the Park Service. How did he say that? He said he didn't think the United States of America was so poor that it couldn't have these areas, nor so rich that it could do without them. He was a wonderful man.

J: Is there hope, do you have hope, for the things you envision?

M: I suppose. I'm always saying at these speeches I give that I'm a born optimist and maybe I'm an optimist because I'm a coward. Maybe I'm just not brave enough to really look the facts in the face. But even if I felt that none of these lovely things were going to take place, it would still be more interesting to me and more fun — that's what I say to these young people — it's better to be in the fight than standing in the corner with your face to the wall, no matter how it may turn out. It's better to be in it.

October 1985
Denver, Colorado

CANYONLANDS NATIONAL PARK

CHAPTER 4

THE CHOICE: REDEFINING THE QUESTIONS

Man sees a reflection when he looks at nature — that part of him he loves, that he cherishes and celebrates in his history and tradition. Yet he simultaneously sees his place in this world — the land is vulnerable to him, but he is as vulnerable, on an individual scale, to the unforeseen: to the quirks or rhythms of a sudden blizzard on a summer's afternoon in the mountains or to a voracious electrical storm stranding him on a peak. He sees his relative youth in trees that have lasted millenia; he witnesses his relative impermanence in canyons carved by forces that are far more consistently powerful than man has yet to be and has yet to understand. In Nature, man sees that his existence in the face of Nature's long consistency is only as the mouse is to his own domain: from the world on the ground, all that we can see we assume to be our kingdom. Yet compared to the force of nature, our kingdom may only be a three by three yard plot of grass. We can choose to live with Nature — the land that supports our past, present and our future — but we cannot choose to live without it. Our understanding of Nature may be the only thing smaller than ourselves in its face.

Understanding is the foundation for choice. In land policy, understanding is the investment we make to assure a choice for ourselves and for the future of the nation. America's natural resources were the reason the country was set apart historically from others in wealth and potential. Continued management of this wealth that is wise, judicious and conservative, in the sense of the first definition in the dictionary,[1] is not a luxury of our modern, high technology civilization. It is a necessity.

Hopefully by now, the lands in which you and I have partial ownership and in which our vital interests rest, have more texture and color in our minds' eyes and have less the amorphous sense of the abstract notion that accompanies the term "public land." The lands themselves are real and vibrant. They are the material that form both the roots and the future of this country, providing the substance that sustains our national wealth and which nurtures our dreams.

Hopefully as well, the issues facing the future of our country's lands are a little better understood. The future is nothing more than last night's dreams and fears, on the one hand. Yet the future is reliant upon our ability to mix those dreams with understanding of the real situation, to create action that will make of our lives — and thus of the lands upon which we rely for the necessities of life — that which we want for ourselves as a people. The future, as always, is in a great part up to us, the collective trustees of the country in which we live. It is a fallacy to think that the future of these public lands is *not* within our guidance. Each of us probably has some sense of what we would like to do with our inheritance and with our tangible wealth; the public lands are but a part of this sense of personal wealth that accompanies such choice. It is in our best interest to ask ourselves what we would like the future to be and how the land — private or public — is affected in our meeting those objectives and goals.

It is equally a fallacy to believe that the future — especially concerning our nation's natural resources — belongs only to our children and thus that the problems of land policy we create today can be left for them to work out. They can do no more than work with the material we give them and must use the logic or illogic of our actions to guide their thinking and policy-making. We are only robbing our own piggybanks in assuming that an unidentified "other" is making our national public land policy and is taking judicious care of our national wealth. We would not entrust our own bank accounts or our children's trust funds to an undetermined decision-maker, so why do we do so with our natural resource? The best definition of democracy is that it is an expression of the commonality of our hearts, based on informa-

tion, intellect and understanding, as well as an intuitive sense of
what is right for us as a people. It demands participation from
each of us, if not in the actual shaping of land use philosophies,
then at least in our informed participation in management direction set out by policy leaders. To leave it to these unidentified
"others" to decide our future use of our land violates our democratic sense and right of purpose and participation.

Had "others" such as Jefferson or Roosevelt, Zanhiser,
Murie, Udall, McCall or McGee, in the past abdicated from trying to set land-use national objectives and philosophies, our
sense of national wealth today would be greatly changed. It
would probably have diminished in equal proportion to the waste
we would have made of the land and thus of our wealth of natural resources. Such a concern was true 100 years ago, as George
Perkins Marsh noted in 1864:

*"Man has too long forgotten that the earth was given to him for usu-
fruct alone, not for consumption, still less for profligate waste. Nature
has provided against the absolute destruction of any of her elementary
matter, the raw material of her works; the thunderbolt and the tornado,
the most convulsive throes of even the volcano and the earthquake,
being only phenomena of decomposition and recomposition. But she
has left it within the power of man irreparable to derange the combinations of inorganic matter and of organic life which through the night of
aeons she had been propostioning and balancing, to prepare the earth for
his habitation, when, in the fullness of time, his Creator should call
him forth to enter into its possession."*[2]

The land, and use of our natural resources, will be of concern 100 years from now, for as Abraham Lincoln said, the only
real, lasting wealth of a country is its lands. Land is land, public
or private, the difference resting only in who makes the decision
as to its fate — preservation or use, wasted or locked up, abused
or put away, managed, conserved, preserved, or invested — depending on one's point of view. Is there a value existing in "public lands," with ownership remaining in the undefined abstract of
"public domain," "government," or "federally managed?" Or is
the best use of the land accomplished by entrusting its management to private ownership or non-profit conservation boards that

*T*he rough riders have never exer-
cised themselves over much about the future, or about any considerations except economic ones. They don't conceive that they owe the future anything, and neither did their grandfathers: hence the half-ruined
natural endowment of the West that we have inherited. What agitates
the bird watchers is something that the rough riders cannot even comprehend; it is the absolute reverse of narrow self-interest; it is the hope
that by work and by renunciations, in their coming age of steel and
concrete and plastic and crowding and the accumulating carbon com-
pounds of human and automotive waste, some humble notion of what
it is to be a man, an evolved mammal, part of the natural world.

Wallace Stegner
*The War between the
Roughriders and the
Birdwatchers*
1964

have as their sole purpose to carry out the public will for the lands of the nation's wealth?

Another way to ask the question is whether there is something within us, as Americans, that needs to know that there is publicly-owned land — i.e. land that we all own? In asking the question, we should momentarily leave aside the questions of the quality of current, federal management. Would the national parks inspire as much pride if they were being operated and owned by a non-profit preservationist-mandated group rather than by being public land, managed by a public agency?

One of the worst by-products of public ownership is the broad brush, single objective approach to management. All too often, the federal agencies apply this approach across the ecological board to varied ecosystems and to the variety of biological and topographic realities that exist in areas ranging from the Arctic tundra of Alaska to the rain forests of the Pacific Northwest to the deserts in California to the high, arid, alpine Rocky Mountains. Yet it is the nature — and arguably the necessity — of public agencies to manage for the "norm," for there is neither manpower nor, more importantly, incentive — economic or ideological — to manage for the specific and unique needs of each parcel of public land.

Anyone who thinks about the differences of a forest in the Pacific Northwest versus the Rocky Mountains would easily recognize the different management needs of such diverse biological units for their best cultivation and use. Individuals within the agencies do recognize the different needs of these ecological areas, but they are roped into broad management and policy objectives that are applied to this diverse land like shellac. The result is that the Rocky Mountains are expected to produce the same amount of timber as the thick forests of the Pacific Northwest, despite the fact that you or I could tell the difference between a four-foot thick tree in the Northwest that grows in 60 to 70 years compared to the Rocky Mountain two-foot thick pines that require 125 years to grow in the Rockies. Recognizing the difference in biological regions is key to good management. To ask the purpose of using the resource in the first place is manda-

tory if management is ever to improve. The sooner we abandon
the mentality that because the resource is there, we must use it,
the sooner we begin to approach true stewardship of our natural
resource wealth.

The second problem with public ownership is the public's
tendency — our tendency — to feel as if we have little to do with
the way our lands are being managed. If we take seriously the
intent of the acts creating most of the public lands — and I see no
reason not to do so — then as beneficiaries, it is our choice and
responsibility to participate in management and planning by
asking ourselves two questions: 1) How do we want to use the
lands and 2) What do we want from the land in the future? Is it
not time to make these agencies of service listen to the people
rather than just the organized special interests? Is it not in each of
our vital interests to be interested in how our future is being in-
fluenced, especially when the beauty and pride we feel as Americans stems from our land?

Pride in ownership is the key to our natural resource future.
If we strip away the jargon and politically-loaded terms such as
"wilderness" or "multiple use," we find that most of us can and
do agree on how we would like to see our natural resources
used. Others' experiences in negotiations over public-land use
bear out this encouraging notion. As we saw in the last chapter,
many different voices speak of the purpose and the means of
management of the public lands, but the visions and ultimate
goals are similar. The "public" in public lands is us and now is
the time to see where we stand on the values of public-land use.

For each of us to endeavor to answer the five questions
posed to the participants in the last chapter would be a start in
defining our own interests and goals for the future of our natural
resources. Then maybe we should ask the questions of our local
resource managers — the forest rangers we meet on a weekend
hike, our local BLM service officers on the range, the next national park ranger or wildlife refuge officer we meet — in order
to compare and better understand how the environment around
our homes is being managed. Our own answers may be personal
or possibly more a feeling than an opinion easily expressed in

words. Chances are that our answers to these questions will be more a sense of hope for the continued wealth inherent in wise and judicious stewardship of our natural resources and public lands. It might be a hope similar to that which the early founders of our country must have felt as they forged a new understanding of government, and similar to the hope they felt as they placed their trust in the people to recognize their own best interests.

•What do you perceive to be the value of the public lands?

•What, in your personal opinion, is the best use of the public lands?

•What will be the purpose of the lands in the future? What will be their role?

•Look one hundred years into the future. What is the view that you would like to have of the public lands? What is your vision for them?

•From that position one hundred years hence, look back at our generation. Judge or assess that which you see as public land policy today. What will people say about our management? What would you change?

What would each of us be missing if the lands that we know now as public and available to each of us — the Yellowstones, the grazing lands, the forests and deserts, the energy and minerals, the Alaskan tundra — didn't exist in the public domain? Imagine for a moment what it would be like without these places accessible to us for outings by car, foot or armchair travel. Are the public lands as rich to us as a concept — an internal space or state of mind in which we can individually nurture our sense of freedom and wealth as a country — as they are in reality as a place we may visit once or never during our lives?

*T*here *is as yet no ethic dealing with
man's relation to land and to the animals and plants which grow upon
it. Land, like Odysseus' slave girls, is still property. The land-relation
is still strictly economic, entailing privileges but not obligations . . .*

*The land ethic simply enlarges the boundaries of the community
to include soils, waters, plants and animals or collectively: the land.
This sounds simple: do we not already sing our love for and obligation
to the land of the free and the home of the brave? Yes, but just what and
whom do we love? Certainly not the soil, which we are sending helter-
skelter downriver. Certainly not the waters, which we assume have no
function except to turn turbines, float barges, and carry off sewage. Certainly not the plants, of which we exterminate whole communities without batting an eye. Certainly not the animals, of which we have already
extirpated many of the largest and most beautiful species. A land ethic
of course cannot prevent the lateration, management and use of these "resources," but it does affirm their right to continued existence, and, at
least in spots, their continued existence in a natural state. In short, a
land ethic changes the role of Homo sapiens from conqueror of the land-
community to plain member and citizen of it. It implies respect for his
fellow members and also respect for the community . . .*

*Land then, is not merely soil; it is a fountain of energy flowing
through a circuit of soils, plants, and animals. Food chains are the living channels which conduct energy upward; death and decay return it to
the soil. The circuit is not closed; some energy is dissipated in decay,*

some is added by absorption from the air, some is stored in soils, peats, and long-lived forests; but it is a sustained circuit, like a slowly augmented revolving fund of life. . .

An ethic to supplement and guide the economic relation to land presupposes the existence of some mental image of land as a biotic mechanism. We can be ethical only in relation to something we can see, feel, understand, love, or otherwise have faith in . . . It is inconceivable to me that an ethical relation to land can exist without love, respect, and admiration for land, and a high regard for its value. By value, I of course mean something far broader than mere economic value; I mean value in the philosophical sense . . .

To sum up: a system of conservation based solely on economic self-interest is hopelessly lopsided. It tends to ignore, and thus eventually to eliminate, many elements in the land community that lack commercial value, but that are (as far as we know) essential to its healthy functioning. It assumes, falsely, I think, that the economic parts of the biotic clock will function without the uneconomic parts. It tends to relegate to government many functions eventually too large, too complex, or too widely dispersed to be performed by government. An ethical obligation on the part of the private owner is the only visible remedy for these situations . . .

A land ethic, then, reflects the existence of an ecological conscience, and this in turn reflects a conviction of individual responsibility for the health of the land. Health is the capacity of the land for self-renewal. Conservation is our effort to understand and preserve this capacity.

Aldo Leopold
A Sand County Almanac
1949

For most of us, the public lands may have little to do with our daily duties and thus their value may seem obscured or be relegated to thoughts about the future. For those whose livelihoods are reliant upon the land — the rancher and energy-developer alike — their perspective might not be very different when it comes to looking at the value of public land. I wonder if the way the rancher perceives the land while looking out over the range is really any different than the perception of the coal company executive? In both cases, the perception is colored by their reliance upon temporary production, this season, this year, this generation, this business cycle. A rancher would argue that he considers the next generation in his use of the land, but so would the coal company operator at a different point in his operation. In the same vein, does the off-road vehicle user or motorcyclist driving over the deserts of California really have any different perception of the lands as a place for recreation than the backpacker or hiker, especially when entertaining the questions of personal responsibility and personal investment in the future of those lands?

What is it we value, that gives us a sense of wealth that we want to pass on to another generation? What is it that draws the five million visitors to Yellowstone each year? If each of those visitors were not partial owners of the park, would the value and enjoyment be the same?

Searching for the answers to these questions will lead all of us closer to creating a statement of a land ethic. Don't let the term "ethic" in this age of "use-it-now" close your mind to the concept. Moving forward without a land ethic is like the colonies declaring war on England without having written a Declaration of Independence. An ethic is but a statement of belief, a conscious understanding and expression of our hopes and desires for the future, for our lives, and for our actions regarding the land. It places our hopes into a pro-active state rather than reactive, in that we remove the land from status as a passive object and recognize it for the importance it plays in our lives: the land is the future, and an ethic about its use is simply a statement of our intent and goals for use. Where would we have been in 1776 without a Jefferson to put into words our collective gripes and hopes? It was a statement — the Declaration of Independence — that led to action; it remains an expression of hope that we cling to yet today. Can we not do the same for the land that has enabled us to enjoy the fruits of our freedom and self-determination in such relative wealth? Creation of a land ethic now is late, but not too late, for there is no hope like that which we hold today for tomorrow.

In the final analysis, for most of us, the lands we share play a dual role: they supply the physical foundation for the wealth of our country, both in tangible and intangible terms; and they are a pallette for our values as a people. We can preserve them, work them, use them, manage them, or ignore them and ignore the future use of them, but no matter what we do or don't do to them, our actions say everything about us as a people.

Our public lands reflect our thoughts and our wisdom, or our failings and our ignorance of our relationship with the land around and under us as the foundation of our society. Neither of these roles need to be recognized or acknowledged by us to be effected by us; our very insistence on proceeding forth without managerial or philosophical goals of what we want from this land of wealth is proof enough that land policy takes place whether or not we take an active part in the policy design.

The fact that some wilderness or national parks actually do exist reflects that we have valued something in ourselves and in our nation. That we set aside some of the land we sought to master so that others, later on, could assess its greatest value, serves as a reflection of our pride in ourselves as Americans. When others, later on, assess our land policy, they will be assessing us, our era and our generation, at the same time.

The fact that we have left some lands aside for time alone to dictate their ultimate use reflects our recognition of an uncertain future. It reflects our recognition of our simultaneous impotence over the future and equally of our destructive potential as a species. To the extent that our public land policies reflect on us as a people should stir our collective egos sufficiently for us to develop a conscious land-use philosophy or ethic. Why are we allowing our own voices to be lost or ignored? Why are we permitting a *defacto* land policy — the result of our individual apathy — to write our history?

It was inconceivable to the people of the United States in 1872 that the land around Yellowstone — wilderness in its truest sense at the time — would ever be anything other than a wild and unnamed land. That today, a park concession system that meets the needs of millions of visitors would exist would have been beyond the wildest dreams of those who set it aside. Yet for us today, the park is a playground to which we go to recreate, to play, to enjoy quiet and to enjoy a sense of nature simply as it exists. The same is true for the other national parks around the west, and of Alaska in general, where nature simply exists and where we humans can return to our pasts and our futures at once by witnessing the forces of nature.

Neither can we know today, nor predict in the future, the resulting impact these forces will have on the land. Our wildest dreams today may indeed be the common reality of tomorrow. But there is a difference between dreams and planning, fantasy and anticipation, hopes and intent and design. If we are to have that which we value today to contribute to the history of the future, then we must take the time to create a tangible consensus on the goals we hold as a people.

As we have seen, the agencies in their near-hundred year histories have been sensitive to the voices of the people. The agencies are magnified reflections of the prevailing philosophies and attitudes of both the era of their creation and, to a lesser extent, the currents in the tide of land policy today. In each of the cases of major land policy — the Louisiana Purchase, the creation of the parks and forest agencies, the grazing service, the wilderness system and Alaska's lands acts — there were a few leaders who helped the country to understand the source of its collective wealth and helped to form the policies of the time. These policies may not have worn so well with age, or the demands of our present era may have changed the objectives for land use. But the complaint that we need to change federal land policy does not speak as loudly as the fact that we still have a

*H*ow long shall this nation endure? *Or, more exactly, how long shall human beings occupy this land? It is only within the past two centuries that the lands of the country have been subject to agriculture upon an extensive scale, and the main drafts upon the soil of this country have been within the last century. We should think, not of a hundred years, nor of a thousand years, but of hundreds of thousands, or of millions of years of development of the human race. There is no reason, from a geological point of view, why human beings may not live upon this earth for millions of years to come, perhaps many millions of years, and, so far as we are concerned, such periods are practically infinite.*

These considerations impose upon us as our most fundamental duty the transmission of the heritage of our naural resources to our descendants as nearly intact as posible . . . We may hope that the scientific advance will help in reference to some of these resources, but we cannot hope that we shall be able to reverse the great law that energy is run down in transformation, or that we can re-use indefinitely the resources of nature without loss.

Charles R. Van Hise
World's Work
1909

choice of how to use our natural resources. We still have options in creating new policies that fit our philosophy of land use,
that will meet the needs of the present and will provide the aura
of hope and resources for those in the future. If we today want to
more fully participate in the design of our land policy and in the
creation of the future goals for our national wealth, we can be
assured of having an impact.

Ironically, action can also be a negative side effect of our interest in our public lands, if action leads us to loving the lands to
death. Along with interest in our land's future must come an understanding of the effect of our visits and our uses of the lands. I
think Rod Nash said it best when he noted that, "Clearly it is not
wilderness, but people who need management."[3] This understanding of our impact is a sign of a society coming of age, of
our maturity to plan and dare to take control of our destiny rather
than relying upon the impetuousness of youth. The youth of this
country in the 1800s served to provide the energy to explore, the
recklessness to dream, and the enthusiasm to believe and attain in
those dreams in the lands of brighter destiny of the frontier. Our
maturity as a people is required now, as we seek the judicious-
ness of being conservative, again in the first definition of the
word, with our land and our natural resources.

I suspect that there is no greater sense of impoverishment
for the American people than to have their land degenerate in
value and beauty before our eyes. Joseph Sax captured the argument for all of the public land agencies when he observed about
the National Park Service that,

*"Most conflict over national park policy does not really turn on whether
we ought to have nature reserves (for that is widely agreed), but on the
uses that people will make of those places — which is neither a subject
of general agreement nor capable of resolution by reference to ecological
principles . . . The National Park System and other bureaucracies that
manage nature reserves are also basically reflective institutions. Strictly
speaking, they enforce the rules Congress makes, doing what they are
told . . . But no administrative agency is in fact so mechanical in its
operation. It has its own sense of mission, an internal conception of
what it ought to be doing and that sense of mission also harks back to
what thinkers have persuaded it, institutionally, to believe."[4]*

It is within our power to participate in our land management policy and it is in each of our individual best interest that we raise our voices to participate in that sense of mission.

The greatest threat to our American public lands is simply our apathy — or worse, our studied ignorance — toward the choices and issues that we have before us. These choices and decisions determine the future of our land and thus our future as a people.

Without our interest, our lands and natural resources will be mishandled by our myopia for only our present needs. Our federal servants will continue to do the bidding of the land use philosophies of the past or seek to manage our resources thinking they are doing the best for us now, in the present. The danger of our ignorance is that we will allow our natural resource wealth to be squandered through policies that no longer fit our philosophy of need nor match our wishes for use of these lands. Our silence will be taken — or mistaken — for agreement with their goals; the result will be a barren future.

As we, the people, accrue the benefits from the land — as we bask in our pride of ownership and feel wealthy because of this land — we also gain an implied responsibility: our participation. Our future is in these lands — our lands of brighter destiny — and the future of the land is simply our choice.

END NOTES

CHAPTER 1

1) In the course of the negotiations over the Louisiana Purchase, it was argued that new states that would be created out of the wild western territory would probably not want to join the new Union. Jefferson acknowledged the argument, countering, ". . . Is it not better that the opposite bank of the Mississippi should be settled by our own brethren and children, than by strangers of another family? With which shall we most likely to live in harmony and friendly intercourse?" (Second Inaugural Address, March 3, 1803 (pg 518)). He also maintained the view in a letter to John C. Breckenridge on August 22, 1803, saying, ". . . It is the elder and the younger son differing. God bless them both, & keep them in union, if it be for their good, but separate them if it be better." ((pg. 1138)) Both taken from *Thomas Jefferson, Writings,* The Library of America, (Literary Classics of the U.S., New York, NY 1984).

2) Interview with Sally Fairfax, Associate Professor of Resource Policy Law, College of Natural Resources, University of California, Berkeley. 1984.

3) Numbers and statistics from the Public Land Statistics, 1983, U.S. Department of Interior, Bureau of Land Management, U.S. GPO.

4) ibid.

5) Report of the Forest Service, Fiscal Year 1983, U.S. Department of Agriculture.

6) Tom Arrandale, "Rocky Mountain West: An Unfinished Country,": in Editorial Research Report, Vol. I, No. 10, Congressional Quarterly, 1980.

7) Letter from Thomas Jefferson to John C. Breckenridge, Aug. 22, 1803, Text taken from *Thomas Jefferson, Writings,* op.cit.

8) A desciptum of the settlement of the west, and the economic pressures, as well as the sense of adventure can be obtained from Ray Allen Billington's *The Far Western Frontier, 1830-1860,* (Harper & Row, Publishers, New York, 1956).

9) Interview with Professor Fairfax.

10) For good histories of the Louisiana Purchase and Jefferson, I recommend Dumas Malone, *Jefferson the President, First Term, 1801 - 1805, Volume 4,* of a set on Jefferson (Little Brown and Company, Boston, 1970) or Bernard DeVoto, *The Course of Empire,* (Houghton Mifflin Co., Boston, 1952).

11) Letter from Thomas Jefferson to John C. Breckenridge, Aug. 22, 1803. op.cit.

12) FABRICUS in Boston Columbian Centinel, July 13, 1803, taken from Dumas Malone, *Jefferson the President, Vol. 4.* , (pg. 297, Little Brown and Company, Boston, 1970)

13) Taken from the Introduction to the *Journals of Lewis and Clark,* Edited by Bernard DeVoto.

14) Abraham Lincoln, Second Annual Address to Congress, December 1, 1862.

15) Theodore Roosevelt, "Opening Address by the President." Proceedings of a Conference of Governors in the White House, Ed. Newton C. Blanchard (Washington, D.C., GPO, 1909) included in (pg 49) *The American Environment, Readings in the History of Conservation,* Ed., Roderick Nash, (Addison-Wesley Publishing, Reading, Mass. 1976).

16) Statistics taken from Public Land Statistics, 1983, BLM.

17) Notions of increased value of the land were included in Ray Allen Billington, *The Far Western Frontier,* (Harper and Row, 1956).

18) Marion Clawson, *The Federal Lands Revisited,* pg. 21 (Resources for the Future, Washington, D.C., 1983).

19) Marion Clawson notes that Thomas Jefferson suggested the cadastral — rectangular — survey for the nation's land, which created the 640 acre section, one mile long on each side, and able to be equally divided into four quarter-sections, which dominated the era of public land settlement. (pg 21) *The Federal Lands Revisited,* (Resources for the Future, 1983).

20) Clawson lists Roy M. Robbins, *Our Landed Heritage: The Public Domain 1770-1970* (2nd Edition, Lincoln, Univ. of Nebraska Press, 1976), as well as Paul Gates, *History of Public Land Law Development,* written for the Public Land Law Review Commission (Washington, D.C., GPO, November 1968). Professor Fairfax notes Samuel Hays, *Conservation and the Gospel of Efficiency* (Cambridge, Harvard University Press, 1959). I would like to add to the list, her book, Samuel T. Dana and Sally K. Fairfax, *Forest and Range Policy* (McGraw-Hill, New York, 1979) among others. While not dealing specifically with the public lands, the series of the New American Nationa, Ed. Henry Steele

Commager, and Richard B. Morris, to which Billington's *Far Western Frontier* is a part, is enjoyable reading. (Harper and Row, Harper Torchbooks).

21) *The Wonders of Yellowstone,* Ed. James Richardson, pg. 130 (Scribner, Armstrong and Company, New York, 1874).

22) ibid, pg.3.

23) Interview with Sally Fairfax.

24) W.J. McGee, "The Conservation of Natural Resources, " cited in *The American Environment, Readings in the History of Conservation,* Ed., Roderick Nash, (Addison-Wesley Publishing Company, REading, MA, pg. 45, 1976.).

CHAPTER 2

Section I — The Forest Service

1) Interview with Sally Fairfax, Univ. of California, Berkeley.

2) Harold K. Steen, *The U.S. Forest Service,* A History, University of Washington Press, Seattle, 1976.

3) Wengert, Dyer and Deutsch, "The Purposes" of National Forests — A Historial Re-Interpretation of Policy Development," is a great document from Colorado State University in which original research into the importance of water rights in the national forests is fleshed out with testimony from the time. Colorado State University, Fort Collins, 1979. All of the quotes from the debates on establishment of the Forest Service are taken from this gem.

4) Cited in Wengert, Dyer and Deutsch.

5) Paul Russell Cutright, *Theodore Roosevelt, The Naturalist,* (Harper Press, New York, 1956).

6) William O. Douglas, taken from *Voices for the Wilderness,* Ed. David Brower, A Sierra Club Book.(Sierra Club. Ballantine Books, New York, 1969.).

7) Glen O. Robinson, *The Forest Service,* (Resources for the Future, Johns Hopkins Press YR).

8) ibid.

9) See the GAO Report on timber sales, 1983.

10) Barney Dowdle, in *Bureaucracy Versus Environment,* John Baden and Richard Stroup, Editors, (University of Michigan Press, Ann Arbor, 1981).

11) William F. Hyde, *Bureaucracy Versus Environment*, ibid.

12) Wenger, Dyer and Deutsch, op.cit.

13) Letter of Gifford Pinchot, in Wenger, Dyer, Deutsch, op. cit.

14) Joseph L. Sax, *Mountains Without Handrails,* (Univ. of Michigan Press, Ann Arbor, 1980).

15) Steen, op.cit.

16) Paul Russell Cutright, op.cit.

Section II — The National Parks, Wilderness and Refuges.

1) Paul Russell Cutright, op.cit. in Forest Service notes.

2) Lt. Doane is quoted in the report on Yellostone National Park, *The Wonders of Yellowstone,* (Scribner's 1874).

3) William C. Everhart's history of *The National Park Service_*was both informative and entertaining and highly recommended reading.

4) ibid.

5) ibid.

6) Interview with James. B. Thompson, Superintendent of Rocky Mountain National Park.

7) Ranger was quoted in Everhart, op.cit. Bob Ferris, a retired National Park Ranger, voiced almost the exact quote in his interview.

8) Everhart, op.cit.

9) *National Parks for the Future: An Appraisal,* The Conservation Foundation, Washington, D.C. 1972.

10) ibid.

11) Everhart, op.cit.

12) Roderick Nash, *Wilderness and the American Mind*, 3rd Edition, (Yale University Press, New Haven, 1967) Nash has written an incredible and

interesting history of the thought toward wilderness that says as much about us as a people as it does about land policy. I greatly appreciate his help and his opening his thoughts to me for the book.

13) David Brower, *Voices for the Wilderness,* Ed. Wilham Schwartz, (Sierra Club. Ballantine Books, New York, 1969.).

14) Rod Nash, interview.

15) Nash, op.cit.

16) ibid.

17) Theodore Roosevelt, *Autobiography,* op. cit.

18) U.S. Fish and Wildlife Service, Regulations and Charter establishing.

19) Interviews with the National Park Service — Alaska.

20) David Brower, *Voices for the Wilderness,* op.cit.

21) Joseph Sax, *Mountains Without Handrails,* op.cit.

22) National Parks for the Future, op.cit.

Section III — The Bureau of Land Management

1) Phillip O. Foss, *Politics and Grass,* (University of Washington Press, Seattle, 1960).

2) ibid.

3) Foss and economist Gary Libecap both make the point in their books.

4) Gary Libecap, *Locking up the Range,* Pacific Studies in Public Policy, Pacific Studies in Public Policy (Ballinger Publishing, Cambridge, MA, 1981).

5) Foss, op.cit.

6) Libecap, op.cit.

7) Foss, op.cit.

8) *Public Land Policy,* Proceedings of the Western Resource Conference, (University Press, Boulder, 1968).

9) BLM Charter, in Marion Clawson, The Bureau of Land Management, (Praeger Library of U.S. Government Departments, New York, 1971).

10) Farry Carpenter, in Foss. op.cit.

11) Clawson, op.cit.

12) Libecap., op.cit.

13) Clawson, op.cit

14) ibid.

15) ibid.

16) ibid.

Section IV — Alaska

1) *Facts on Alaska*, 1985 edition, (Alaska Northwest Publishing Company, Anchorage).

2) *Wilderness and the American Mind,* Nash, Op.cit.

3) ibid.

4) Interview with Jay Hammond.

5) U.S. Congressional Testimony.

6) Interview with Morris Udall.

7) *Facts on Alaska*, op.cit.

8) See USFS Annual Report and the GAO Report on timber cutting

9) *Facts on Alaska,* op.cit.

CHAPTER 4

1. Conservative: "1. conserving or tending to conserve; preservative, to keep from being damaged, lost or wasted; save..." *Webster's New World Dictionary, Second College Edition.*

2. George Perkins Marsh, *Of Man and Nature,*   Ed. David Lowenthal, (Belknap Press, Harvard Univ. 1965)

3. Rod Nash, interview.

4. Joseph Sax, *Mountains Without Handrails*, op.cit.

SELECTED BIBLIOGRAPHY

Billington, Ray Allen, *The Far Western Frontier 1830-1860* (Harper and Row, Publishers, New York, 1956)

Clawson, Marion, *The Federal Lands Revisited*, (Resources for the Future, Washington, D.C., 1983)

Clawson, Marion, *The Bureau of Land Management*, (Praeger Library of U.S. Government Departments, New York, 1971)

DeVoto, Bernard, *The Course of Empire*, (Univ. of Nebraska Press, Lincoln, 1952)

Everhart, William C., *The National Park Service*, (Westview Press, Boulder, 1983)

Foss, Philip O., *Politics and Grass,* (University of Washington Press, Seattle, 1960)

Jefferson, Thomas, *Writings*, The Library of America (literary Classics of the U.S., New York 1984)

Leopold, Aldo, *A Sand County Almanac,* (Oxford University Press 1949)

Libecap, Gary, *Locking Up the Range*, (Pacific Studies in Public Policy, Ballinger Publishing, Cambridge, 1981)

Malone, Dumas, *Jefferson the President, First Term, Vol. 4,* (little Brown and Company, Boston, 1970)

Nash, Roderick, *Wilderness and the American Mind,* (Yale University Press, New Haven, 1967)

Public Land Statistics, 1982, 1983, 1984, U.S. Dept. of Interior, Bureau of Land Management, US GPO

Robinson, Glen O. *The Forest Service,* (Resources for the Future, Johns Hopkins Press)

Steen, Harold K., *The U.S. Forest Service,* (Univ. of Washington Press, Seattle 1976)

Sax, Joseph L., *Mountains Without Handrails,* (Univ. of Michigan Press, Ann Arbor, 1980)

Wengert, Dyer and Deutsch, *"The Purposes" of National Forests — A Historical Reinterpretation of Policy Development,* (Colorado State University, Fort Collins,1979)

The American Environment, Readings in the History of Conservation, Ed. Roderick Nash (Addison-Wesley Publishing, Reading, 1976)

Bureaucracy Versus Environment, Ed. John Baden and Richard Stroup, (Univ. of Michigan Press, Ann Arbor, 1981)

The Journals of Lewis and Clark, Ed. Bernard DeVoto, (Houghton-Mifflin, Boston, 1953)

Voices for the Wilderness, Ed. David Brower, (Sierra Club, Ballantine Books, New York, 1969)

The Wonders of Yellowstone, Ed. James Richardson (Scribner, Armstrong and Company, New York, 1874)

INDEX